# PATHFINDER HISTORY

# Russia under Lenin and Stalin

## Dean Smart

*Series Historical Consultant:*
Dr R.A.H Robinson,
The University of Birmingham

Stanley Thornes (Publishers) Ltd

First published in 1998 by: Stanley Thornes (Publishers) Ltd, Ellenborough House, Wellington Street, CHELTENHAM GL50 1YW, England

98  99  00  01  02  /  10  9  8  7  6  5  4  3  2  1

A catalogue record for this book is available from the British Library.

ISBN 0 7487 3485 6

Illustrated by Hardlines, Charlbury, Oxfordshire

Printed and bound in Great Britain by Redwood Books, Trowbridge, Wiltshire

Typeset by Tech-Set Ltd, Gateshead, Tyne and Wear

## Acknowledgements

With thanks to the following for permission to reproduce photographs in this book:

Corbis UK Ltd, p.32; David King Collection, pp.9, 11, 15, 17, 22, 27, 28, 39, 45, 46; London Evening Standard, pp.45, 51 (Source 4); School of Soviet and Eastern European Studies, University of London, p.49.

Every effort has been made to contact copyright holders. The publishers apologise to anyone whose rights have been inadvertently overlooked, and will be happy to rectify any errors or omissions.

# Contents

# *How to Use this Book*

History at A-level is a more complex and demanding subject than at any preceding level, and it is with these new and higher demands on students in mind that the Pathfinder History series has been written. The basic aim of the book is simple: to enable you to appreciate the important issues that underpin understanding of the principal factors in the nature of Russia before, during and after the 1917 Revolutions, under Lenin and Stalin.

What this book does not do is provide a single source of all the answers needed for exam success. The very nature of A-level study demands that you use a range of resources in your studies, in order to build up the understanding of different interpretations on issues, and develop your own argument on exam topics. Pathfinder can help make this subject more accessible by defining the key issues, giving an initial understanding of them and helping students to define questions for further investigation. It concentrates on the fundamentals of Communism and the Soviet state; the important issues, events and characters of the period that you must understand, and which the examiners will want to see that you know.

Hence it becomes more of a guide book to the subject, and can be used whenever you want within the A-level course; as an introduction, as a reminder revision text or throughout the course or module each time a new topic is started. Pathfinder also has several important features to help you get to grips with the history of Communist Russia to 1953.

The book follows the three basic stages of the A-level process, explaining why they are important and why you are doing them. The three sections of the book are thus Overview, Enquiry and Investigation, and Review. These describe the main methods for studying history at A-level; so, for example, when you answer a question on Stalin's totalitarian style and domestic policy, you will recall how this book approaches the topic with these three headings in mind.

## KEY ISSUES AND KEY SKILLS

Pathfinder is written around three basic principles. The first is that it covers the most important events, themes, ideas and concepts of the subject called the *Key Issues*. The second is that there are levels or tiers to these issues, so that a major question is broken down into its contributory questions and issues and is thus easier to understand. And the third principle is that there are fundamental skills that you must develop and employ as historians at this level, and these are referred to as *Key Skills*.

These principles combine in Section 1, where **The Big Picture** sets the whole scene of the topic and identifies the most important periods and events within the topic. **The Key Issues** establishes what the author believes are the fundamental questions and answers to the subject as a whole, and then analyses these in more detail by raising all the contributory questions contained within the main question. Each period is discussed in more detail in Section 2, and you will see page references for each appropriate chapter. Each period thus also has its own issues and concepts, to provide a second tier of Key Issues. Finally, the **What to Read, how to Read, where to Find it and how to Use it** section offers hints and advice on the active study skills that you will be using in A-level history.

The main focus of the book is Section 2, called **Enquiry and Investigation** because this is exactly what you are being asked to do for most of the time during the A-level process. You are making historical enquiries and learning how to interpret sources and information every time you look at a document, analyse a photograph or read around a topic. Each chapter takes as its title one of the periods identified in The Big Picture, and each one also identifies what you need to bear in mind when working on that particular issue or theme. There is a useful little tab at the start of each double-page spread which summarises the most important aspects of the topic and identifies the skills that you will use in studying it.

These are Key Skills, although you could think of them as key study skills if you prefer. There are a number of them, and they can be grouped under the following headings and with these helpful definitions:

## Skills for collecting information from historical sources

Analysis: breaking down information into component parts (making notes under section headings, for example).

Interpretation: considering the implications of information and cross-referencing to other sources or contextual knowledge to develop your understanding further. (Skills used within this are actually inference, deduction, extrapolation, interpolation, recall and synthesis.)

Evaluation: assessing the validity of sources and hence the implications for the reliability of its information.

Recording: arranging information into sections that allow easy retrieval as required. For example making linear notes (good for large amounts of information), diagrams and flow charts or mind maps (good for establishing relationships between sections of information).

## Skills for applying and using information

Explanation: using information to show how and why something happened.

Assessment: weighing up possible explanations or interpretations.

Forming hypotheses: setting up an explanation or judgement for further testing.

Testing hypotheses: using information to support and challenge a hypothesis to improve it

Setting a thesis: using the information to present, support and sustain a tested hypothesis and an explanation of historical processes.

You will see that some skills are flagged more often than others, and there may be others, such as chronology, that are not defined here. However, the important point to remember is that these are the skills that the A-level historian has to have available for use, and that you are actually using them all the time already. The aim is to reinforce these skills for you, and to enable you to see how you are using them and why.

**Section 3 Review** then brings all the interpretations, investigations and issues that you have looked at on Soviet Russia into one place. **Synthesis** is the bringing together of issues, arguments and judgements into overall answers. It also poses answers to what the author considered to be the main issues identified in Section 1. **Argument** then takes the information, knowledge and hypotheses and applies them to building up explanations and producing more detailed essay answers, of the style you might find or you might write in an exam. The **Final Review** is something of the author's own thoughts and conclusions to the subject on a broad level.

## MARGINS AND ICONS

Pathfinder divides material as part of the main aim of focusing attention on the most important issues. Hence the main central narrative discusses and interprets information and, although detailed, cannot provide all of the information on its topic. The narrative can be integrated and supplemented with more detailed works, articles and documents.

All other sorts of information appear in the margins and you will see the following icons used alongside them. Not all icons appear in every chapter and some chapters have other features included as well, but the icons should help you manage the extra information given on topics:

 Documents, historiography and sources – quotes from texts, individuals and passages

 Suggested headings for notes

 Suggested further reading

 Sample activities and exam-style questions

 General hints, study tips and advice

 Key words

### Who were the Russians?

Minority ethnic groups within the Russian Empire:

| Nationality | Millions |
| --- | --- |
| Russian | 55.6 |
| Ukrainian | 22.4 |
| White Russian | 5.8 |
| Polish | 7.9 |
| Jewish | 5.0 |
| Kirghiz | 4.0 |
| Tartar | 3.4 |
| German | 1.8 |
| Latvian | 1.4 |
| Bashkir | 1.3 |
| Lithuanian | 1.2 |
| Armenian | 1.2 |
| Romanian/Moldavian | 1.1 |
| Estonian | 1.0 |
| Turkmenian | 0.3 |

*From H. Macdonald, Russia and the USSR, Empire of Revolution, 1994*

# The Big Picture: Russia 1917–1953

## THE ROAD TO REVOLUTION

History, according to Edward Gibbon, 'is little more than the register of th crimes, follies and misfortunes of man'.

Twentieth-century Russian history might largely fit into Gibbon definition, with millions sacrificed to incompetence, ideology, ambition an greed, autocracy and revolution, dictatorship and extremism. Yet the stor of the Russian people during this century has been one of undoubte hardship and success against the odds, and we must not always judge by th standards of the day alone, or miss the moments of victory and heroism.

This was also a century of economic and political progress, of a grea political ideal – of equality for all and that the state operates to benefit th people. Although Russia became a world power, wrongs were done an ordinary people were sacrificed to ideology. As we approach the end of th century, we can begin to look back. Was Gibbon right? Remember that w look as outsiders, and that we must seek out the everyday acts of self-sacrific and heroism, the nobility and integrity, and remember that Russia is still vast, multinational and diverse mass of individuals. We look at individua and not the Russian people as a whole.

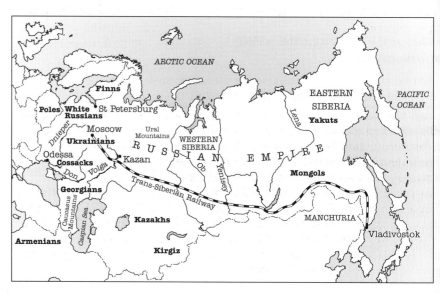

*Russia before the Great War*

## LOST OPPORTUNITIES – THE 19TH CENTURY

The Romanovs spent decades, largely unsuccessfully, trying to modernis their Russian Empire. Each Tsar and Tsarina quickly realised that Russia' massive size and problems made reform not only unlikely but impractica Serious reform would inevitably affect vested interests and cause disquiet i one or more sections of the population.

Despite attempts on the lives of several Tsars, only Alexander II wa assassinated, in 1881. Having survived one assassination attempt in 1866 he had clamped down for a while, and ironically was eventually assassinated as he relaxed his control and considered reforms. He was succeeded by hi

Alexander III (1881–1894) and his grandson Nicholas II (1894–1917). either man has been seen by historians as a successful ruler. C. A. Kent, in *European History 1789–1914*, dismisses them both as 'narrow minded d of limited intelligence'. Nicholas led Russia in a disastrous war against an, faced revolution in 1905 after 'Bloody Sunday', and committed ssia to the Great War (1914–1917), which resulted in enormous vastation and loss.

## 917 – A YEAR OF REVOLUTIONS!

### hat was the Impact of the Great War?

1917, the 'quick' war had dragged on for three years and both sides were ar to exhaustion. The war was to cost 1.7 million Russian dead: it vastated much territory, weakened Russia's economy and ultimately ntributed to the feeling of hardship and injustice that led to the 1917 volutions. For Russia, 1917 saw revolution, armistice and withdrawal from e war in early 1918.

### he Events of 1917

here were two revolutions in 1917. The first was in February 1917. Why then? By 1917, the war was going badly, having caused shortages and high sses. The Brusilov Offensive failed and the Russian army neared haustion and mutiny. At home there were bread and anti-war riots: otesters expressed their concerns more vociferously and public order gan to decline.

The result was that Nicholas II abdicated, and the Provisional vernment was formed.

### ow did the Provisional Government do?

itially popular, the government consisted of many parties that wanted fferent things, from moderate to radical reform. They refused to end the ar, believing that they could win it! Shortages and hardship worsened. The vernment had loosened restrictions on criticism and disbanded the Tsar's cret police. In the cities, criticism of their actions became intense.

In July 1917, there were substantial mutinies amongst front-line troops; July the Army's Commander-in-Chief looked as if he would attempt a ilitary coup, and the Bolshevik Party attempted to use the situation to force e overthrow of the Provisional Government. They failed and their leaders re either arrested, escaped or went into hiding for a time. Lenin went road, but only to nearby Finland.

### he October Revolution: 'Peace, Bread and Land'

the war continued, the Bolshevik slogan of 'Peace, Bread and Land' must ve seemed very attractive to many Russians. Throughout the autumn the lshevik leadership debated whether Russia was ready for a workers' volution. Lenin returned to Russia secretly, and the Bolsheviks awaited eir opportunity. Their chance came on 7 November. On a signal of the ing of the guns of the battleship *Potemkin*, they took control of Petrograd. enin and his colleagues then set up a committee to govern, and began to nvince the urban workers that they were the right and only government for ssia.

Winning the hearts and minds of the working classes in the rural areas uld come later!

### Place names

St Petersburg, Russia's second city – renamed as Petrograd during the Great War – was later renamed again as Leningrad. In 1991, the name St Petersburg was restored.

Stalingrad was renamed Volgograd in 1961, after Stalin had been denounced as a tyrant by Khrushchev at the 20th Party Congress in 1956.

### A note on dates

When you read about the events of the Russian Revolution, it can be confusing. Dates in different books and documents appear to disagree, because two different calendars are being used.

Before 1918 the Russians were using the Julian calendar, which calculated the date 14 days behind the Gregorian calendar that was used by the rest of Europe!

Be careful with dates before 1918. At its simplest level, on the Russian calendar the Bolshevik Revolution happens in October 1917, but for Westerners it happens in November.

In February 1918, the Bolsheviks adjusted the Russian calendar. For Russians, there was no 1–13 February 1918!

### Russia's problems in 1917

The Empire was:
- Large, with poor transport and communication
- Multicultural
- Based on an agricultural economy and infrastructure
- Beginning to urbanise and industrialise
- Inefficiently run by a weak autocratic government, helped by a conservative upper class
- Fighting, and losing, a war

### THE KEY ISSUE

The development of the Soviet state under Lenin and then Stalin

### THE KEY SKILLS

Investigation
Explanation: events
Awareness of key issues and questions

### WHAT YOU HAVE TO DO

Use the key issue to get an overview of the main events and people, and of the issues that are raised by historians. You need to understand the philosophy behind Communism, and be aware of the international tensions that conflicting political systems cause.

*radical* – a person who seeks considerable change, often looking to remodel society or its institutions
*reformer* – a person who seeks to change a system, rules or laws, usually in a peaceful way
*revolutionary* – a person who plots to overthrow the established system or government to gain radical reform: the revolution itself can be either violent or peaceful
*capitalist* – a person who believes in a free market, and private ownership of wealth
*Communism* – the idea that the wealthy exploit the workers, and thus will be overthrown, developed in the 19th century by a German Jew, Karl Marx: such ideas meant that Marx was not welcome in most European cities, and he settled in London

## THE ROAD TO DICTATORSHIP

To take command, the Bolsheviks established systems to control the arm the navy and the civil service, and mechanisms for regulating the peop New legislation began the process of creating a Communist state. One their first actions was to re-establish a secret police. They did not ha majority support. A Civil War began, which would last until 1921: t eventual Bolshevik victory was secured partially due to the failure of the opponents to work together and organise an effective joint campaig Prominent Bolsheviks took charge, with Lenin as leader.

Chapter 2 examines the actions of the Bolshevik government, and the consequences are explored in Chapter 3, which examines the Civil War.

## THE STRUGGLE FOR SUCCESSION BEGINS

In 1924, after illness and a series of strokes, Lenin died. A power strugg ensued as Josef Stalin, the General Secretary of the Communist Party, beg to edge Leon Trotsky, Minister for War, out of office. He removed Trotsk supporters and by 1929 was undisputed leader. Chapter 4 examines t power struggle and its consequences.

## HEAVY INDUSTRY

Stalin believed that careful planning by the state would overcome a obstacles, and he tolerated no delays or difficulties. Any serious failure achieve the targets was attributed to deliberate opposition and sabotage, a those responsible were arrested. The plans concentrated on heavy industri coal, iron and steel, oil and electricity, and communications. Targets we unreasonably high, and although historians disagree about the accuracy production figures, enormous steps forward were made.

The USSR needed to develop its industrial capacity and create infrastructure for commerce and trade, and communications and transpo In order to develop heavy industries, armaments and agricultur equipment, a series of Five Year Plans were introduced, with clear targe and expectations. When the 1929 global economic depression began, Russ was partially shielded due to its limited contact with the outside worl Chapter 5 explores the role of statistics in informing the historian, focusir on the Five Year Plans.

## STALIN IN CONTROL

To develop agriculture, collectivisation of farming was proposed, und which peasants who owned private land pooled crops and animals in larg state-run collectives. The wealthier peasants, or *kulaks*, resisted this, an many thousands were arrested and executed, or interned in labour camps, *gulags*. Before any results appeared, there were famines and millior suffered and died.

Stalin has become notorious for using terror to crush opposition. Durin the 1930s, the secret police ruthlessly eliminated opposition: the leadershi and key roles in the administration were purged of all but unquestionir Stalinists. Hundreds of thousands were sent to labour camps, into intern exile, or sentenced and executed in show trials. Chapter 6 looks at Stalir domestic policies and autocratic rule, and Chapter 7 focuses on the use propaganda and the development of a personality cult based around Leni and Stalin.

Between the wars, the Soviet Union was treated with distrust by the oth international powers. Remember that the USSR had withdrawn from t Great War in 1918; that some of the Communist leadership had advocate encouraging revolution elsewhere; and that many of the European states ar the Americans had intervened, on the losing side, in the Civil War. It is not surprising therefore that relations were frosty.

Things worsened with the rise of fascism in Italy, under Mussolini, and in Germany, under Hitler. As Germany rearmed, Stalin prepared for war, but despite opposing political beliefs Hitler and Stalin signed the Nazi Soviet Pact, on 23 August 1939. This guaranteed that neither state would fight the other, and they secretly agreed to carve up neighbouring territory. It seemed that Germany and the USSR would not have to go to war. Chapter 8 looks at the USSR's relations with other states from 1928 to 1941, and the impact of isolation and mistrust.

## THE GREAT FATHERLAND WAR

As the Second World War began in September 1939, the Soviet Union remained neutral, but used the opportunity to invade and seize part of Finland. In 1941, Hitler's forces made war on the USSR. Fighting on the Eastern front was intense and the USSR lost much land to early successful German advances. Only at enormous cost were the Germans contained at Stalingrad, and then pushed steadily back. Although the combined effort of the Allies defeated fascism by 1945, relations between Russia and the other Allies were often strained. Approximately 20 million Soviet citizens died as a result of the war, and countless others were displaced, desolate and dispossessed. Chapter 9 looks at the war, with an emphasis on its cost, and the impact on the Soviet people and their attitudes.

As 1945 saw the new age of the atomic bomb, Stalin used newly 'liberated territory' between the USSR and the West to create a buffer zone. The uneasy alliance of war quickly became the mistrust of the Cold War.

## THE COLD WAR

During the war agreements had been made to ensure that British, French and American forces did not accidentally fight Red Army forces as each side liberated Nazi-occupied territory. The result was that each side effectively occupied half of Europe. Countries such as Poland, Hungary, Bulgaria and Romania were rapidly turned into Communist states, and two armed camps developed, as the capitalist and Communist countries engaged in an arms race. This fierce competition between ideologies caused near catastrophe, as conflicts across the world were encouraged or caused by capitalist and Communist rivalry. Chapter 10 looks at the Cold War and its consequences.

## THE GREAT DICTATORS?

*Karl Marx, 1818–1883*

Lenin and Stalin shaped the lives – and took the lives – of millions of people in their own country and beyond. Can Karl Marx ever have imagined what Communism in Russia would mean? This book attempts to put the events and personalities into context, to explore issues in a little more depth, and to suggest sources for further information and research, as well as looking at the way in which historians have reacted to the Soviet era.

### Interpretations

There are two classic approaches to interpreting Soviet history:

'The interpretation of the Bolshevik Revolution that became established in the Soviet Union in the 1930s and remained enthroned at least until the mid 1950s might be described as formulaic Marxist. The key points were that the October Revolution was a true proletarian revolution in which the Bolshevik party served as the vanguard of the proletariat, and that it was neither premature nor accidental ...'

'In the West Soviet history became a matter of strong interest only after the second world war, mainly in a Cold War context of knowing the enemy ... the totalitarian model ... was the most popular interpretative framework. It emphasised the omnipotence of the totalitarian state and its levers of control , paid considerable attention to ideology and propaganda, and largely neglected the social realm. Most Western scholars agreed that the Bolshevik Revolution was a coup by a minority party, lacking any kind of popular support or legitimacy.'

**Sheila Fitzpatrick, *The Russian Revolution*, 1994**

For an overview of the period covered here, and a review of the changing historiography of the Soviet era, see David Christian, *Imperial and Soviet Russia* (Macmillan Press, 1997), Sheila Fitzpatrick, *The Russian Revolution* (Oxford University Press, 1994) and Richard Pipes, *A Concise History of the Russian Revolution* (Harvill Press, 1995).

# The Key Issues

Listed here are some of the key issues that historians discuss and attempt to resolve. Some are straightforward, and can be answered with factual and objective accounts; others require interpretation and draw on more subjective evidence and opinion. As you build your knowledge of Russian and Soviet history, you might find it helpful to refer back to this list and the accompanying timeline (see the inside back cover) to give you the issues in outline. Individual sections deal with some of the issues in more depth, but to understand the historical debate between historians fully you will have to look at the work of a number of historians.

## 1. LENIN AND THE BOLSHEVIK REVOLUTION

### Pre-revolutionary Russia (see pages 16–19)

- What was Russia like before the 1917 Revolutions?
- Why was there opposition to the Tsar's government?
- Why was there discontent in Russia by 1917?
- What was the impact of the First World War on Russia?

### 1917 – Year of Revolutions (see pages 16–23)

- What were the causes and consequences of revolution in Russia in 1917?
- Why, when and how did the February 1917 Russian Revolution take place?
- Was a revolution inevitable by 1917? (This is one to discuss.)
- Why did the February Revolution succeed when earlier revolutions failed?
- Why did the Tsar abdicate?
- What were the results of the February Revolution?
- Was the Provisional Government doomed to failure? (One to discuss.)
- Why was there a revolution in October 1917?
- How did the Bolsheviks gain and consolidate power in October 1917?

### Bolshevik Russia, 1917–1924 (see pages 20–27)

- What changed in Russia under the Bolshevik government?
- Who were the leading Bolsheviks?
- Who supported the Bolsheviks?
- Why were there elections which were then cancelled?
- Why did the Bolsheviks take Russia out of the Great (First World) War?
- What impact was there in withdrawing from the Great War?
- Why were the Russian Royal Family (the Romanovs) murdered? Was this justified?
- Were the Bolsheviks right to be ruthless?
- Why was there a Civil War, and what was its impact? (One to discuss.)
- What was War Communism?
- What propaganda and other tactics did the Bolsheviks use to convince their own people that they were right?
- What were international relations like in the early years of Bolshevik rule?

### The Role of Lenin (see pages 28–29)

- What was Lenin's role in the October Revolution and Bolshevik government and later development of Russia?

What sort of man was Lenin?
To what extent did he cause the October Revolution?
How did he shape Bolshevik Russia?
Was Lenin a dictator?
How was a personality cult created around Lenin?
Who were the possible 'heirs to the revolution' after Lenin?

# . THE STALINIST ERA

## rom Russia to the USSR, 1924–1928 (see pages 30–31)

Why, and with what consequences, was there a power struggle after Lenin's death in 1924?
Who were the key figures of post-Leninist Russia?
Was Trotsky a better revolutionary than Stalin?
Lenin wrote that he didn't trust Stalin – yet Stalin became leader. How and why?
Was the New Economic Policy good for the Soviet Union?

## talinist Russia, 1928–1953 (see pages 32–41)

What was it like to live in Stalinist Russia?
What changes did Stalin make?
How did Stalin change the economy of the USSR?
What were the Five Year Plans, and were they a 'Great Leap Forwards' for the Russian economy?
What was the 'Great Terror' and what were the purges? Were these policies justified?
Was dictatorship inevitable?
How and why did Stalin build a personality cult around himself?

## oreign Affairs, 1928–1953 (see pages 42–53)

What was the USSR's relationship with the outside world like between 1928 and 1953?
With what justification did the Communist leadership mistrust and fear the West?
What were relations like between Russia and the West from 1928 to 1941?
What was the impact and legacy of the 'Great Fatherland War' from 1941 to 1945?
What impact did Stalinist Russia have on its neighbours and the West?
What legacy did Stalinist foreign policy leave for Russia and the world?
To what extent did Stalinism shape Russia in the years after Stalin?

## valuating Lenin and Stalin: What do the Historians Say? see pages 60–61)

What have historians said about Russian and Soviet history in the past?
What are their views now?
What sorts of evidence are available from the Soviet era?
Why and how are interpretations changing?
Will we ever be able to get a full picture of the Bolshevik and Stalinist years in the USSR?

### Vladimir Ilyich Lenin, 1870–1924

V. I. Lenin (originally Ulyanov) was the Bolshevik leader in 1917. He was educated at the universities of Kazan and St Petersburg, where he gained a law degree. He was imprisoned for revolutionary activities from 1895 to 1897; exiled to Siberia from 1897 to 1900, and in 1903 caused the split in the Russian Social Democratic Labour Party that created the Mensheviks and Bolsheviks. He spent 1905–1917 abroad, returning after the 1917 February Revolution from Zurich to Petrograd. He led Soviet Russia from 1917 to 1924. On his death, Petrograd was renamed Leningrad, and his body was embalmed and placed in a mausoleum in Red Square, until removal and burial in 1994.

## THE KEY ISSUES

- What do you need to know about Russia and the Soviet Union in the 20th century in outline?
- What do you need to know in depth?

## THE KEY SKILLS

Research skills
Communication
IT: databases, Internet, word-processing, DTP

## WHAT YOU HAVE TO DO

Decide what you need to know. If you don't know what you need to know, ask.

If you are studying Russia and the Communist era, find out *exactly* which topics you have to study – which in outline and which in depth. It will be important to ensure that you prioritise, and that you concentrate on reading about the things that you definitely need to know.

From the variety of books available in libraries and bookshops, pick those that seem clear and that deal with the general or specific topics that you want. All books are written for specific intended audiences, so some books will go into more depth than you need. Have a good look before you buy anything.

# What to Read, how to Read, where to Find it and how to Use it

## 1. WHERE TO FIND INFORMATION

You might find it helpful to begin by gaining an overview of 20th-century Russian history, so that the key events and names begin to fall into some sort of order, and then begin to build up some in-depth and more detailed knowledge.

Overviews are best obtained by looking at either a straightforward text, or by using a summary in one of the many revision or study guides available. Often the more recent encyclopaedias and CD-ROM encyclopaedias or history disks have excellent summaries. Not only are the CD-ROM encyclopaedia histories of Russia easy to read and understand, but most can be printed off, or can be sent to a word-processor program or stored on disk, and then can be edited. Getting familiar with modern communication technology is worth the investment of time and effort, which will be repaid in full. When you are more confident you might also want to trawl through the Internet, which can be an excellent source of information, interpretation and discussion, and increasingly has superb on-line resources from academic archives, museums and other places.

When you have achieved a reasonable understanding and have some idea of who was who, you might feel more confident to engage with the more detailed account of the past and begin to look at more analytical and discursive work, but do not be afraid to go back to the overview to put things into their broader context, and to maintain your understanding of the wider issues if you need to check where specific events fit into the scheme of things.

## 2. GETTING A BALANCE

It is easy to be absorbed by Russian history and look at the events in isolation without reference to the international scene and world events. The 20th century has been a particularly turbulent time for Russia and the world, and you might want to keep an eye on international affairs, as they undoubtedly influenced much of Russian domestic policy as well as the relationship with the outside world.

A number of history books include a helpful chronology of national and international events, and will allow you to see what was going on in the wider world or within Russia. In this book, Section 1 provides an overview and chronology to put issues into their context, and Section 2 discusses some of the key issues of the topic. Where space allows, new terms are explained and put into context throughout the book.

## 3. OVERVIEW TEXTS

To find out what happened during the 20th century in Russia fairly briefly, look in book or CD-ROM encyclopaedias, or in works of general history. General works of history are also useful: look for something that deals with Russian history clearly and in a straightforward way. Don't be afraid to use bits of several books, and reject anything that you find confusing or unclear. Ask a friendly librarian or history teacher for ideas if you can, and get the basic 'what happened when, and who are the key names' sorted out.

## . OTHER SOURCES

istory is not just written in textbooks. There are many different academic
urnals and magazines which might just have the very article that you are
oking for. Again, teachers and lecturers might be able to recommend things –
it they are often too busy to keep really up to date with what has been written
nd published on every topic. Go to one of the larger libraries that stock a range
f magazines, and see what you can find. Remember to ring up first to find out
hat historical magazines they have – they won't read the contents to you over
ie telephone, but at least you will know that there is something there.

## . INFORMATION TECHNOLOGY (IT)

on't be afraid to use new technology to save yourself time and make yourself a
:tter and more informed learner.

Most British and American CD-ROM encyclopaedias are worth trawling to
ain an overview of the period, and will give you a general coverage of main
vents and personalities from the leadership. The approach will be easy to read
nd understand, because the texts are written for a large and broadly based
idience. There will be limited depth and no attention to the historical debate
r to issues that are subject to historiography and interpretations that historians
iake (which means that some issues are fiercely debated by historians, and
ieir viewpoints differ). Do not expect to find much attention to this except in
ie more specialised texts, although they are most unlikely to cover specific
vents in any detail.

Trawl the Internet as well. It takes a little while to find out how to 'surf the
eb', and it does take a while to find relevant sites, but it can provide fantastic
ee (apart from the cost of the phone bill) sources.

## . WHERE TO READ

ou need to read somewhere quiet, with a good light, and when you are calm.
Research into learning shows that concentration spans reduce over time, so
e realistic: don't try to read for more than an hour at a time. Blocks of about an
our are best, with a short break in between if you are really concentrating –
ightly more if you want to get an overview.

## . WORKING AT THE COMPUTER

he computer is a marvellous device, but use it for study – not for games! Don't
pend more than about 45 minutes at a screen without taking a short break, and
o remember to save your work periodically to prevent losing it.

## . USING THE INTERNET

s the Internet develops, more and more useful resources are becoming
vailable. Begin with simple searches using key words such as 'Lenin' or 'Stalin',
nd as your confidence increases try more complex searches and see what
esults you can achieve.

xcellent sites can be found at the following addresses:
*The Library of Congress Soviet Archive*, at
`http://www.ncsa.uiuc.edu/SDG/Experimental/soviet.exhibit/so`
`viet/archive.html`
*The Stalin Archive*, at
`http://acs.bu.edu:8001/~sbern/note.htm`
(apart from the Stalin material, this site has excellent links to socialist sites)
*Bucknell University Russian Department*, at
`http://www.bucknell.edu/departments/russian/russian.html`

---

**For effective reading:**
- Get an overview:
- What happened in the period in general?
- What were the key events?
- Who were the key personalities and names?
- Find out about the chronology in a bit more depth:
- What was happening inside Russia?
- What are the key foreign events that shaped thinking?
- Find out about the key events and related issues:
- What specific things happened and why are they considered important?
- How do the different events and issues fit together?
- What aspects of this topic do historians argue and disagree about?

---

### Internet research

There is a lot of useful information in the *Stalin Archive*. Or try this Finnish Internet site:

`ftp://ftp.funet.fi/pub/culture/`
`Russian/html_pages`

contains useful images of propaganda art under both Lenin and Stalin, as do several other sites.

Alternatively, try an Internet search using 'Lenin' or 'Stalin', and see what you can find!

## THE KEY SKILLS

Research skills
Self-review
Critical awareness

- History is shaped by the age in which it is written Historians agree on facts, but can differ on interpretations.
- The range of sources used to write history shapes the result.
- Different sources are available at different times in history.
- The date at which research and writing is done can influence the outcome.

### Schools of history

Historians are good at putting people into pigeon-holes. We do it all the time – Tudors, Stuarts, Scots, Russians ... We also do this to each other. In the past two centuries, historians have created the notion of *schools of history*, by which they mean that historians exhibit certain characteristics in their writing and have certain attitudes towards the past and history.

Ask your teacher or lecturer if they can recommend writers from different schools of history. This will give you different perspectives on the past and will help you to see that history is far from a dry account of facts and dates.

# A Guide to Reading

## 1. USING YOUR TIME EFFECTIVELY

Have you ever stopped to think about how effectively you do some of the things that you do every day? Do you reflect on how well you use your time

You probably don't – or certainly not very often. Just like all of the people in history before us, we are too busy living our lives to draw breath and sto and reflect, but looking at how well you work can be very valuable. Th section is an attempt to make you think about the different purposes reading – and how to work in a smarter way, rather than just harder!

If you use the time that you have to work effectively, you will see significant improvement in your understanding, your knowledge an perhaps even in your grades. To begin with, think about what you read, wh and how.

## 2. READING WITH A PURPOSE

There are several *different* reasons for reading.

### Reading to gain an overview

We have already looked at the idea that it is easier to get to grips with subject if you have a fairly sound general idea of what happened when, wh the key players were and what the outline results are for the big events. Th book attempts to provide you with the 'big picture' and then looks at issue in more detail.

In some ways it doesn't matter which sort of book you start off with here as long as it's accurate. Start off with something simple, and work up t in-depth articles and texts as your general knowledge improves.

### Reading for detailed coverage

When you have a sound understanding of the general events of a period, it important to begin to fill in a more advanced understanding. Very fe people would expect you to sit down and read whole books. It is much mor productive to mix and match, reading one or two chapters out of a certai work, and looking at another text to fill in the gaps and provide othe information. If you are really serious about understanding any subjec properly, you should look at least two different texts. Librarians will be abl to tell you what they have on your chosen subject, and lecturers and teacher might have a good idea of which bits of which texts are good and easy to rea – use other people's expertise and experience, but do also dip into thing and see what you think of them.

### Reading to answer a 'big' question

If you have to find out information to write an essay, to respond to question or to look at some sort of factual issue and respond to it, it is worth thinkin through exactly what you need to know. By all means read for pleasure, bu it is a different approach from reading for data.

Home in on texts using their title. Are they on the right subject? Do the cover the right period?

Look at the contents and the index – and flick through. Select texts tha seem to explain clearly and concisely, but that do support their reasoning You want to be able to develop your own opinions – not just be told what t write. Use overview texts to help to define the key issues of topics.

## Reading for interpretations and to understand historiography

As your knowledge builds, you will begin to see that although historians might agree about certain key facts and events there are often major disagreements about what the facts mean. It is possible to come up with very different conclusions about the rate of change, development and continuity; about the nature and role of individuals; about the key features of a period and the things that influenced the times, and so on.

## Attitudes and availability

Historians also carry a lot of personal baggage with them. Their past experience and awareness, their attitudes and their beliefs will shape the way in which they write and interpret the past. This does not imply sinister motives and biased reporting of the past, but that history is fragmentary – the record of the past is incomplete, and much requires interpretation. It is also important to remember that the sources available to different historians will vary. Regional and state statistics and archives, especially for the Soviet Union, will present different versions of the past, and of course before the collapse of the USSR much documentary material was not available to Soviet writers, let alone Westerners!

## Reading for reference

There are times when you need to check a date, fact or name. Perhaps you came across something in a book, or a name popped up in a document. The fastest way to find out is to use a small reference book or historical dictionary. Some excellent ones are available: for example, Collins Gem offer *Basic Facts 1900–1980* at pocket size; Longman have a *Handbook of Modern European History* which is about as big as a large novel; and many other publishers offer handy desk-sized reference volumes.

Don't buy the first one that you see straight away! Have a quick flick through and see if the book has good coverage and includes what you want. Does the volume offer lots of concise clear information? Is there coverage for the period that you are studying? Try looking at the entries for 'Lenin' and 'Stalin', and then check something more specialised, such as 'Comintern' or 'Zinoviev'.

## 3. DEVELOPING AN AWARENESS OF SOURCES

There is nothing to stop photographers and propagandists from creating the image they want; interfering with negatives; and altering the way in which pictures are printed, cut or presented. This is a classic example of the way in which a photograph can be retouched to alter the image.

*Lenin addressing a crowd of troops: Moscow, 5 May 1920*

*A Stalinist era release of a photograph of the same event*

You will also need to look at a variety of primary source evidence and develop an awareness of the strengths and weaknesses of different types of source.

## THE KEY ISSUES

- What were the long- and short-term causes of the Russian Revolutions of 1917?
- What was the Russian Empire like?
- What were Russia's problems?
- Why was there an attempted revolution in 1905?

## THE KEY SKILLS

Overview and chronology
Analysis: causation
Communication

## WHAT YOU HAVE TO DO

List the things that you would *expect* might cause a revolution, and then the things that a sensible government might do to stop revolution. Now look at the events that really took place. Did you get right the reasons for discontent and the government's attitude?

---

## Nicholas Romanov, 1868–1918

As Nicholas II, the last Emperor of Russia, he reigned from 1894 to 1917. His grip on power weakened after the Russo-Japanese War (1904–1905), the 1905 protests and failed revolution. He was forced to set up a Duma – a weak parliament that increasingly demanded reform. He declared war against Germany and Austria–Hungary in 1914 and took personal command of the army in 1915, and thus was personally blamed for the military disasters. He was executed, with his immediate family and servants, by Red Guards at Yekaterinburg in 1918.

---

# *Why Russia? Why 1917?*

At the start of the 20th century, Russia was an Empire of many nationalities and religions, languages and beliefs, and was spread across Europe and Asia. It rested on an inefficient farming economy, with limited industrialisation and mechanisation. Most of the population was rural and depended on the local landowner for employment and housing, although towns had begun to be centres of intellectual activity, often through the universities. Communications were poor, as roads were bad and there were few railways, with only a basic telegraph service between major cities.

The army and navy were run by the upper classes, with a clear and disciplined officer corps, and the church (Russian Orthodox) was a conservative force that supported the ruling classes, although parish priests could see the suffering of the ordinary members of their congregations. Power seemed to be in the hands of the wealthy ruling classes, although many members of the middle classes had become wealthy. Tsar Nicholas II was in charge, helped by the Tsarina, the large Romanov royal family and a sizeable aristocracy. The dynasty had ruled since 1613, and was related by marriage to most of the royal families of Europe.

## HOW WAS SOCIETY ORGANISED?

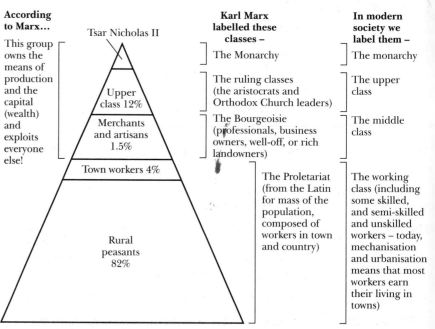

Marx said 'The workers have nothing to lose in this [revolution] but their chains. … Workers of the world, unite.'

## WHY WAS THERE OPPOSITION TO THE TSAR'S RULE?

By 1900, Russia was experiencing considerable problems. Look at the following list of short- and long-term problems. Historians attribute a varying amount of significance to each, and also focus increasingly on regional variations, movements and trends. Traditionally, Nicholas II has been seen as a weak Tsar and therefore at best part of the causes of the Revolution, but could the Tsar have done anything to reduce these problems?

- *Poverty*. Most peasants led a life of hardship, poverty and appalling living conditions. From 1900 onwards, a number of uncoordinated rural protests took place.
- *Urbanisation*. Many town dwellers lived in overcrowded and unsanitary conditions. They worked for low pay and in dangerous conditions.
- *Defeat*. In 1904, Russia went to war with neighbouring Japan. Apart from defeats, the war caused shortages, unemployment, price rises and protest.
- *Discontent*. On 22 January 1905, a peaceful protest march of 20 000 was fired on. Hundreds were killed in the Bloody Sunday Massacre, and many lost confidence in the Tsar's ability to reform. Strikes had increased dramatically, risking the economic development of the country and foreign trade.
- *State debt*. The state had borrowed heavily to fund railway expansion, build factories and create a commercial infrastructure.
- *The Great War*. Russia suffered over 1 million casualties in each year of the war, and thousands of square miles of Russian land were occupied. The Russian army, of over 6 million men, was poorly trained and equipped.
- *Failing confidence*. The Tsar began to be identified with the disasters at the front. The Tsarina was German. Left in charge while the Tsar went to command the army, she refused to follow advice from the Duma. Scandals rocked the court and rumours were circulated. People began to lose any remaining confidence in the Romanov dynasty and its supporters.

# EVENTS: 1894–1917

From the accession of Nicholas to the February Revolution

| | | |
|---|---|---|
| 1894 | | Nicholas II comes to the throne |
| 1902 | | Minister of the Interior Sipyagin assassinated by Social Revolutionaries |
| 1904–1905 | | War with Japan gives the Japanese control over Korea and Manchuria |
| 1904 | | Minister of the Interior Plehve assassinated after encouraging anti-Jewish feelings |
| 1905 | 22 January | Hundreds of protesters shot on Bloody Sunday. The 1905 Revolution begins and fails |
| 1905 | | Tsar issues October Manifesto and promises compromise. Duma elected. Despite reprisals by the pro-Tsarist 'Black Hundreds', and executions of revolutionary activists, things calm down |
| 1911 | | Peter Stolypin, the Tsar's Chief Minister, murdered |
| 1914 | August | Russia declares war on Austria–Hungary, with initial victories but then major setbacks |
| 1915 | 6 September | Tsar becomes Commander-in-Chief of the Army and goes to front line, leaving the German-born Tsarina Alexandra in charge |
| 1916 | | Brusilov offensive against Austria, initial gains lost with 1 million casualties. Army near collapse |
| | December | Grigori Rasputin, advisor to the Tsarina and cause of anti-monarchist feeling, is murdered by a group led by Prince Yusupov. He has to be poisoned, shot and tied up before drowning. |

**Alexander Fyodorovich Kerensky, 1881–1970**

Kerensky was leader of the Provisional Government in October 1917. A well-known socialist lawyer, he was appointed Provisional Government Minister for War, and then Prime Minister. He followed moderate policies, and kept Russia in the Great War. During the October Revolution he fled to France, and then to Australia in 1940. In 1946 he went to live in America, where he wrote a number of books about Russia and the Revolution.

'Kerensky, despite an exalted sense of his mission to save Russia, was essentially a go-between and negotiator of political compromises, not greatly trusted or respected, and lacking a political base in any of the major parties.

*Sheila Fitzpatrick, The Russian Revolution, 1994*

## Who are the key individuals?

Historians sometimes emphasise the role of individuals in looking at cause and consequence. To what extent do you believe that single individuals or small groups cause events to happen – or is causation more complex?

## THE KEY ISSUES

- What happened after the March (February) 1917 Revolution in Russia?
- What was the Provisional Government?
- Who were the Bolsheviks?
- Who opposed them?

## THE KEY SKILLS

Research skills: information collection and interpretation
Empathic awareness

## WHAT YOU HAVE TO DO

Find out the policies of the Provisional Government in more detail, and the reasons for its downfall. Would you have recommended that they acted so fairly and openly? If so, why; and if not, how could you justify being more repressive?

For a first-hand account of the Revolution, look at *Ten Days that Shook the World* by John Reed (Penguin, 1977; first published 1919). To get an overview of the events, look at Chapter 4 of Anthony Wood's *The Russian Revolutions* (Longman, 1979).

For in-depth studies, see: John Daborn, *Russia – Revolution and Counter Revolution* (Cambridge University Press, 1991); E. H. Carr, *The Bolshevik Revolution 1917–1923* (Pelican, 1952); Christopher Hill, *Lenin and the Russian Revolution* (Penguin, 1993); and the sections on 'Why did Tsarism Fall?' and 'Why did Bolshevism Triumph' in Richard Pipes, *Three Whys of the Russian Revolution* (Pimlico, 1998).

# 'Ten Days that Shook the World'

## WHAT HAPPENED IN RUSSIA IN 1917?

There were two revolutions – one in March (February according to Russian dates) and a second in November (October by Russian dates). There were also threats of coups, and attempted revolutions and counter-revolutions. The political parties involved in all this were as follows:

- *Social Revolutionaries*. They favoured revolution to reform land ownership, and were a small group despite there being millions of potential supporters. Their opinions on other policies varied, which fragmented the party and reduced their influence. As they largely believed the way forward was to work with the Tsar, their appeal was limited to republicans only.
- *Constitutional Democrats*. They wanted peaceful change, and were mainly made up of the well-educated and better-off townspeople and professional classes. They had little to offer the peasants and were strongest in the population centres.
- *Social Democrats*. Mostly composed of town and industrial workers, this group was influenced by the political writings of Karl Marx. They believed that the system was fundamentally wrong and that drastic change was needed. This would mean extensive reform, requiring the old, vested interests to be removed. In 1903 this group split into two rival but similar groups, the Bolsheviks and the Mensheviks.

Most Russians were not members of any political party, and did not concern themselves with politics.

### THE MARCH UPRISING

Widespread disorder in Petrograd in March 1917 led to calls for the Tsar to be replaced and a more radical form of government be found. In an attempt to quell the disturbances, the military were ordered from their barracks and on to the streets to disperse the rioters. When ordered to fire on the crowds some detachments did, while others refused or went over to the side of the protesters. The rule of order was slipping away, and the members of the Duma and others formed themselves into a Provisional Government. Simultaneously, workers and soldiers who had been part of the advisory council, or Petrograd Soviet, formed a kind of shadow government. On 15 March, the Tsar attempted to pass the throne not to his son, but to his brother. When he refused the crown, Russia became a republic.

### EVENTS: 1917

The spring crisis

| | |
|---|---|
| January–March | The extreme first three months of 1917 causes further shortages |
| 11 March | Troops fire on rioters in Petrograd. President of the Duma Rodzyanko requests the Tsar to 'form a new government that has the support of the people', and warns of the seriousness of the situation in Petrograd. From Military Headquarters at Mogliev, the Tsar dismisses 'fat Rodzyanko's warning' as nonsense |
| 12 March | Mutinies begin in the Petrograd Garrison: one regiment kills its officers and joins the rioters. Formation of the State Duma to replace the Tsarist government, and of the Petrograd |

| 14 March | Provisional Government formed and ministers appointed. Petrograd Soviet issues Army Order No. 1 assuming command of the armed forces, and instructing them to elect representatives |

Soviet of Soldiers' and Workers' Deputies (3000 members, each representing 1000 people)

14 March Provisional Government formed and ministers appointed. Petrograd Soviet issues Army Order No. 1 assuming command of the armed forces, and instructing them to elect representatives

15 March Tsar abdicates in favour of his brother the Grand Duke Michael, who refuses the crown unless it is offered by the Duma

16 March The State Duma meets, and does not offer Michael the crown. Grand Duke Michael steps aside

## WHAT SHOULD THE PROVISIONAL GOVERNMENT DO?

The new government established a liberal series of policies to lead Russia into a new age. They allowed free speech, and did not prevent the Bolshevik Order No. 1 being followed – which created Soviets in the army and navy, and effectively passed control of the military to the Bolsheviks. Lenin's return in April was followed by his decision to persuade all Bolsheviks to oppose the Provisional Government.

A series of crises followed in the summer. Ministers who favoured continuing the war were forced out, a 'big push' offensive resulted in 60 000 Russian dead, and the Provisional Government's popularity began to sink even further. In July it seemed as if there would be a Bolshevik uprising and in August there was a near military coup led by General Kornilov – this was only averted when Kerensky allowed the men he had earlier described as 'German traitors' (the Bolshevik leadership) to return and organise resistance to Kornilov using the Soviets. By September, Trotsky had become the leader of the Petrograd Soviet, and in October Lenin returned to plan the Bolshevik Revolution with Trotsky.

## EVENTS: APRIL–NOVEMBER 1917

From Provisional Government to Bolshevik Revolution

16 April Lenin returns to Petrograd
26 June Mutinies at the front line by soldiers result in General Kornilov becoming Commander-in-Chief
12 July The Provisional Government restores the death penalty and courts martial
16–18 July The Bolsheviks stir up discontent amongst sailors and Red Guards, the 'July Days' revolt is put down by loyal troops and Lenin flees to Finland to avoid arrest
21 July Kerensky becomes Prime Minister under the new government
8 September General Kornilov begins to move troops into position to take Petrograd. Kerensky denounces the 'Kornilov affair' but requires Bolshevik support to defeat the plot. Kornilov and others are arrested
2 October Congress of Soviets, Decrees on Peace and Land
2 November Parliament refuses Kerensky the power to suppress the Bolsheviks
7 November The Bolsheviks storm the Winter Palace and seize power in Petrograd: telegrams are sent to the remainder of Russia, calling on the Soviets to take power
13 November A counter-offensive by Kerensky fails
15 November The Bolsheviks establish power in Moscow

**Was revolution inevitable?**

Historians differ, and you should think about your opinion on this question. What does the following quotation suggest?

'Both in the towns and in the villages the situation was approaching chaos even without the help of Lenin and the Bolsheviks. Of course, they tried to make matters worse ... They sought to reap the whirlwind. They contributed to the breakdown but did not cause it ... Galbraith has said that the man who breaks through a rotting door acquires an unjustified reputation for violence; some credit should be given to the door.'

*Alec Nove, An Economic History of the USSR, 1992*

You might examine The February Revolution – Why? When, and How?, or consider The Provisional Government – Its Aims and Actions, or study The October Revolution – Why? When, and How?

1 'Weak leadership and liberal policies brought down both Tsar Nicholas II and the Provisional Government in 1917.' To what extent do you agree with this statement, and to what extent do you feel that other factors were also to blame?

2 John Reed, the author of *Ten Days that Shook the World*, died in 1920 and was given a hero's burial in Red Square. He was in favour of the Revolution, and his account shows this. Is subjective reporting of the past acceptable?

## THE KEY ISSUES

- What do revolutionaries have to do to hold on to power when they have it?
- Did the Bolsheviks have the support of the people?
- What policies and actions did Lenin follow in the years from 1918 to 1924?

## THE KEY SKILLS

Research skills and investigation
Hypotheses: making and testing
Empathetic awareness
Communication

## WHAT YOU HAVE TO DO

On first impressions, it is clear that the Bolsheviks were undemocratic and unpopular. Is this true? Is it fair? Find out in more detail what sort of pressures Lenin and the Bolshevik leadership were under, and about their policy decisions.

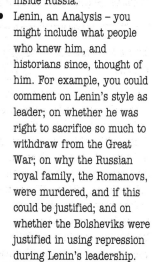

Your notes might address these two issues:

- The Aftermath – international reactions to the Bolshevik Revolution; reactions to the Revolution inside Russia.
- Lenin, an Analysis – you might include what people who knew him, and historians since, thought of him. For example, you could comment on Lenin's style as leader; on whether he was right to sacrifice so much to withdraw from the Great War; on why the Russian royal family, the Romanovs, were murdered, and if this could be justified; and on whether the Bolsheviks were justified in using repression during Lenin's leadership.

# Gaining Power: October 1917

Between 25 and 27 October 1917, the Bolsheviks seized power in Petrograd. They completed a daring coup against an unpopular but liberal government. There were undoubtedly elements of chance in the coup, as well as the influence of key individuals such as Lenin, Trotsky and others. Historians vary on what the events of the Revolution were: their sequence and significance; the extent to which they think that the collapse of the Provisional Government was inevitable; and whether they agree with the Marxist–Leninist theory that a Bolshevik-style coup was inevitable. Since the collapse of the Soviet regime, there has been a move towards disputing previous interpretations of the Communist era. Authors such as Richard Pipes are reinterpreting the past, and he argues that much of what happened was the result of chance and circumstances rather than predetermined planning.

## BOLSHEVIK POLICIES

Efficient firm control of the areas that the Bolsheviks had captured was necessary. Lenin acted quickly to establish his policies. *Land* was given to the peasants, and church land and property was confiscated; *workers* were promised better conditions, and factories and commerce were nationalised; *international debts* were scrapped; *equality* of gender, belief (religion) and race was declared; education and the press were placed under state control; and Soviets were elected to run the workplaces and districts.

The new Bolshevik government negotiated a painful peace treaty with the Germans. The accompanying map shows the resulting loss of land, and thus of resources and population.

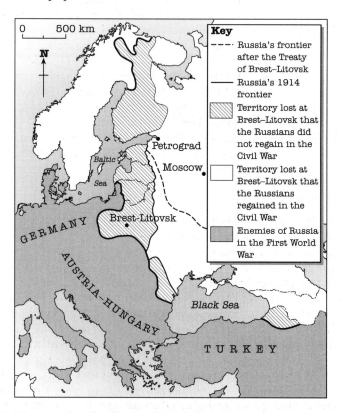

*Land lost by Russia after the Treaty of Brest–Litovsk*

# EVENTS: DECEMBER 1917 – NOVEMBER 1918

The Bolsheviks achieve power

| | | |
|---|---|---|
| 1917 | December | Creation of the *Cheka* secret police; Finland declares independence |
| 1917 | 2 December | The escape of Kornilov and fellow generals from prison in Bykhov |
| 1917 | 17 December | Ceasefire agreed with the Germans and date set for peace negotiations |
| 1918 | January | Creation of the Red Army; legislation on separation of church and state |
| 1918 | 18 January | Constituent Assembly opened, and dissolved the next day |
| 1918 | 1–4 February | Introduction of the Gregorian calendar brings Russian dates into line with the rest of Europe |
| 1918 | 24 February | The Bolshevik government decides to accept the German peace ultimatum |
| 1918 | 3 March | The Treaty of Brest–Litovsk ends the war with Germany on unfavourable terms; loss of Finland, Estonia, Latvia, Lithuania, Russian Poland and the Ukraine |
| 1918 | 12 March | The Bolshevik government moves its headquarters to Moscow |
| 1918 | May | Georgia, Armenia and Azerbaijan declare independence |
| 1918 | 29 May | Partial conscription introduced for the Red Army |
| 1918 | 16 July | Execution of the Imperial family at Yekaterinburg (confirmed by recent DNA test scientific evidence on bones uncovered at the site, although the skeletons of one daughter and of the Tsar's son are missing) |
| 1918 | 2 August | Establishment of anti-Soviet government at Archangel, followed by the landing of foreign troops, and fighting between Soviet forces and troops of the 'White' government and its allies, including USA, GB and Japan. 'White forces' call their government the Directorate, with a capital at Omsk. The Civil War begins |
| 1918 | 13 November | Following the Armistice between Germany and the Allies, the Soviets denounce the Treaty of Brest–Litovsk |

## NEXT STEPS?

In October 1917 the Bolsheviks had captured the capital of Russia, and the mammoth task of capturing the rest of the country lay ahead. Promises and policies had to be made reality once power was consolidated.

Although nominally in power, the Bolshevik government was opposed by other factions and a battle for control of the country began, in what was to be a Civil War that lasted from 1918 to 1921. There was an urgent need to restore at least the semblance of order, and the Communist government set up its own secret police, the *Cheka*, thus reducing the dangerous level of freedom that had enabled them to criticise the previous regime and undermine it to the point of collapse. Although Brest–Litovsk lost Russia about 20% of her land, and payment of reparations to Germany caused discontent within and outside of the party, the transfer of many people into what had been enemy hands and disagreements amongst senior Bolsheviks were seen as a necessary price by the Bolsheviks in giving them freedom to pursue their policies.

---

### What if the different books I read don't agree?

Historians differ in the emphasis they put on certain statistics, sources and documents, so always use at least two good texts to gain an overview of the situation. When interpretations that have been widely accepted in the past are revised, we call this a revisionist approach. A leading revisionist authority on Russia is Richard Pipes of Harvard University (see further reading).

---

To look at what changed in Russia under Lenin, how well Lenin's policies were received, and what the reaction was to the introduction of Communism, see Chapters 4 and 5 of Anthony Wood's *The Russian Revolution* (Longman, 1979) and Chapters 7 and 8 of Michael Lynch's *Reaction and Revolutions: Russia 1881–1924* (Hodder and Stoughton, 1992). These books both take a balanced and clear traditional view of the Soviet era. Then look at Christopher Hill's *Lenin and the Russian Revolution* (Penguin, 1993). For a revisionist view, see Richard Pipes, *Russia under the Bolshevik Regime* (Harvill, 1994).

---

### The ends and the means

Trotsky is alleged to have said 'The end may justify the means as long as there is something that justifies the end' (quoted in A. Pozzolini, *Antonio Gramsci: an Introduction to his Thought* (Pluto Press, 1970)). When you look at how historians report the early actions of the Bolsheviks, consider whether you are being given an objective view or whether value judgements are being made.

# Consolidating Power to 1924

The Bolshevik leadership had not been put into power by the people, and had no mandate from them, so anyone who was not in favour of the Revolution and Communism was a real or potential enemy. The process of finding and removing opposition began. The secret police pressured the opposition to disband or fall into line with official policy. Opposition and free presses were banned, and the detention of thousands of enemies of the state began. The Bolsheviks issued thousands of decrees to change society: industry and land were taken into state ownership, and near anarchy was achieved when the Bolsheviks removed many of the existing structures and regulations of the old society.

From the outside, revolutions can look like cleverly planned unified actions. Historians now agree that the Bolshevik leadership were unable to agree on the date for their Revolution – hence the attempt earlier in 1917 – and even after the seizure of power in October (November) there were still disagreements. Writing in 1993, the British historian Chris Ward said:

'The Bolshevik leaders in power were no happy band of comrades united by a common resolve.'

After the fall of Communism, historians now have access to new documents and are reinterpreting the role of the Bolshevik leaders.

## RULERS OF EVERYTHING THEY COULD SEE

Initially, the Bolsheviks were masters of Petrograd and they then seized other key towns and cities. They only gained control of the countryside gradually. Recent work by historians looks much more at the difference between urban and rural areas at various stages of the Revolution and Soviet era. Some debate is beginning to consider whether rural workers were less active revolutionaries than urban dwellers, and whether the Revolution spread by consent or force.

The Bolsheviks were not a majority party in the Provisional Government, and did not have the support of the majority of the people of Petrograd, although they did have the support of the Petrograd Soviet, and thus the most vocal and active workers, and the army and navy delegates to the Soviet. Lenin formed the Sovnarcom, the Council of People's Commissars, and this group of Bolsheviks ran the country. The Provisional Government had set an election date for November, and these elections took place. The Bolsheviks gained about a quarter of the seats, and the Social Revolutionaries gained an overall majority. The Constituent Assembly convened for the first time in January 1918 – it was only allowed to meet once before Lenin's troops closed the meeting place at the Tauride Palace to the delegates.

*An artist's impression of the execution of Tsar Nicholas II and his family*

## THE KEY ISSUES

- What did Lenin and the Bolsheviks actually do when they were in power?
- How have different historians interpreted the Leninist era, and the effect of the policies?
- Could Lenin's ruthlessness be justified?

## THE KEY SKILLS

Analysis: cause and consequence
Investigation: historical events
Interpretation

## WHAT YOU HAVE TO DO

Investigate the key issues. Was Lenin right to act ruthlessly by looking at the pressures of war, an underdeveloped economy and a lack of democracy, or did he do anything to preserve his position?

*Red Army* – the military forces of the Bolshevik government were known as the Red Army from 1918 to 1946, when 'Soviet' replaced 'Red' in the title

*War Communism* – the Bolsheviks took control of all economic activity employing more than ten people: strikes were punishable by the death penalty; there was massive famine, but the Red Army were fed and supplied

*New Economic Policy (NEP)* – introduced by Lenin in 1921 to counter profiteering and encourage high productivity. Stalin abolished the scheme in 1929

*Cheka (1917–1922)* – the All Russian Extraordinary Commission for Combating Counter-Revolution and Sabotage, established in 1917: in reality, a form of secret police. Renamed on several occasions, it eventually evolved into the KGB

# EVENTS: 1918–1920

Years of turmoil

| 1918–1921 | | During the Civil War, the policy of 'War Communism' is introduced by Commissar for War Trotsky. Ruthless control is exerted over people's lives, and many die; most suffer extreme hardship and malnutrition |
|---|---|---|
| 1919 | March | 8th Party Congress, creation of the Politburo and the Orgburo |
| 1919 | 21 March | The Allies decide to withdraw troops from Russia, finally leaving Archangel on 19 September. Military setbacks increase for the White forces. Omsk is taken by the Red Army on 14 November, with collapse of the White government on 19 February 1920 |
| 1919 | 2–7 May | Establishment of the Politburo and Communist International (Comintern) at Party Congress |
| 1919 | March | 9th Party Congress |
| 1920 | 24 April | The Polish–Russian war begins: the Poles invade the Ukraine, and heavy fighting takes place. Peace negotiations begin on 21 September, with a provisional agreement on 12 October |
| 1920 | March | 9th Party Congress |
| 1920 | August | The Tambov peasant insurrection begins |

# LENIN'S NEW ORDER – HOW RUSSIAN SOCIETY WORKED

The government:
- the Council of People's Commissars
- the Sovnarcom (the cabinet of ministers)

*selected by Lenin*
- Central Committee
- senior government posts

*which elects*
- All-Russian Congress
- a Communist-only parliament
  - ▷ regional elections
  - ▷ district elections

The administration:
- the Orgburo – the Communist department which acts on policy
- the civil service
- the Red Army
- the Soviet Navy
- the Soviet Air Force

The Communist Party:
- the Politburo – the central inner decision-making group

*which elects*
- the Central Executive Committee – which exists to run the Party

*which elects*
- Party Congress
  - ▷ regional Party branches
  - ▷ district Party branches

After 1922, only the Communist Party is legal. Only Communist candidates may stand for election.

## Contradictory sources?

*Source A*

'... there was little arbitrary rule in the period after the civil wars ... the representatives of the old order disliked Soviet Russia as much for the good things as the bad, or perhaps even more.'
**A. J. P. Taylor, From Sarajevo to Potsdam, 1966**

*Source B*

'We stand for organised terror.'
**Felix Dzerzhinsky, leader of the Cheka**

*Source C*

'It is estimated that the Cheka killed more than 250,000 people between 1917 and 1924.'
**Richard Radway, Russia and the USSR, 1996**

*Source D*

'We want to transform the government into an instrument for enforcing the will of the people. We want to organise violence in the name of the interests of the workers.'
**Pravda, 22 November 1922**

The above statements come from British historians, a Russian Bolshevik newspaper and the Bolshevik leader. Do all of the sources support each other? Is it possible that they are all correct? Explain your view.

 For documents, see Ann Bone, *The Bolsheviks and the October Revolution – Central Committee Minutes August 1917–February 1918* (Pluto Press, 1974); Martin McCauley, *The Russian Revolution and the Soviet State 1917–21* (Macmillan, 1975; Document Collection); and John L. H. Keep, *The Debate on Soviet Power* (Minutes of the All-Russian Central Executive Committee of Soviets) (Clarendon Press, 1979).

## THE KEY ISSUES

- Why was there a Russian Civil War?
- How have historians regarded the war in the past?
- How and why is this changing?

## THE KEY SKILLS

Chronology
Interpretations
Reading and evaluation

## WHAT YOU HAVE TO DO

During the Civil War, the Bolsheviks fought half a dozen 'White' armies, nearly a dozen separatist armies and the forces of 14 foreign countries. Establish which factors different historians emphasise to explain Bolshevik victory.

'The Civil War was a rather strange episode in the historiography of twentieth century Russia. It saw an unlikely degree of agreement between Western and Soviet scholars on its origins and the reasons for the Bolshevik triumph. Whereas on most aspects of Russian history in the twentieth century Western and Soviet scholars took diametrically opposite views on how to interpret events, the Civil War witnessed something quite different, Western and Soviet scholars were pretty much at one.'

*Geoff Swain, in introduction to V. P. Butt, A. B. Murphy, N. A. Myshov and G. Swain (eds), The Russian Civil War: Documents from the Soviet Archives, 1996*

Is it better if historians disagree with each other, or would it be more useful if one factual account of the past could be established?

# Baptism by Fire

History re-evaluates the past. Sometimes there is consensus, and sometimes there is disagreement. Very rarely does new material become available to allow a massive reconsideration of the past. From the Bolshevik Revolution of 1917 onwards, outside access to Soviet archives was strictly controlled. Finding adequate primary sources to interpret the past was difficult. Secondary sources were either 'official' Soviet historians – and therefore less critical – or Western, lacking access to a range of sources.

With the collapse of Communism, there has been a sudden and unanticipated increase in access to archives. Historians are able to re-examine the past, reinterpret events and evaluate new evidence. This section looks at the issue of the Civil War, and how interpretations are changing as new evidence becomes available.

## WHY WAS THERE A CIVIL WAR?

Although the Provisional Government had been deeply unpopular, it had not been oppressive. In the summer of 1918, groups opposed to the new Bolshevik government began to organise themselves and prepare anti-Communist counter-revolutions. Those who opposed the Bolsheviks were individuals who stood to lose land and businesses; those who were religious and resented attacks on the power and position of the church; the nobility and ruling classes; the army hierarchy; monarchists and conservatives; foreign powers that stood to gain from a weak Russia; and the many internal nations that saw a chance to achieve self-determination and independence. These formed a natural opposition and were nicknamed 'White forces'.

Across the Russian Empire, as the Bolsheviks struggled to oust the Provisional Government's supporters, new factions and enemies emerged. A bewildering array of forces formed in different areas. British, American and French forces landed at Murmansk and moved south. The Czech Legion, supported by Admiral Kolchak, and British forces fought the Bolshevik forces in the east. In the west there were uprisings in the Baltic states, and the Poles attempted to make gains at Russian expense. To the south-west, the Ukraine and Georgia broke away and sent forces against the Bolshevik armies. The Japanese occupied the Russian Far East until 1922.

The only apparent solution was to present the people with no option but to co-operate. Thousands of hostages and suspected traitors, collaborators and sympathisers were executed without trial. The royal family and their servants, who had been under remote house arrest, were shot and killed. Other bourgeois and upper-class citizens were executed. Waves of terror and bloodshed marked little progress as each side struggled to gain more territory.

## WHY WERE THE WHITES DEFEATED?

The Bolsheviks controlled the centre of Russia and the White forces the extremities. Despite supremacy in numbers, supplies and experience, the White forces were picked off one by one. There had never been any successful coordination between them; their aims and objectives were different, and they could be isolated and despatched. Foreign intervention and support for the Whites, at best half-hearted and sparse, faded away, but left a legacy of bad feeling between the Bolshevik government, their neighbours and the European powers. A number of scores were recorded to be settled later.

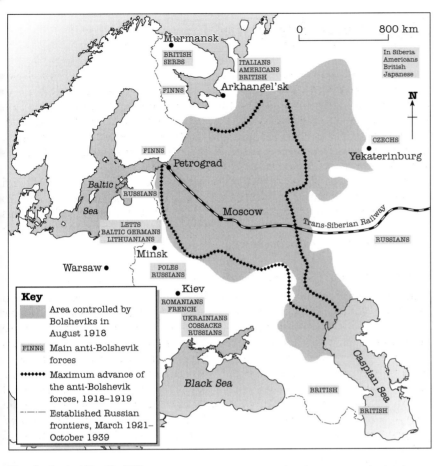

*Russia during the Civil War*

# EVENTS: 1921–1922

Fears of counter-revolution

| | | |
|---|---|---|
| 1921 | February | Workers' unrest in Petrograd |
| 1921 | March | 10th Party Congress |
| 1921 | 1 March | A rebellion at Kronstadt Naval Base begins, following city-wide strikes in Petrograd. Trotsky arrives and puts an ultimatum to the sailors |
| 1921 | 16–18 March | The Naval Base at Kronstadt is bombarded and then assaulted by Red Army forces and opposition is crushed |
| 1921 | 18 March | The introduction of the New Economic Policy replaces War Communism, and allows some private profit |
| 1921 | 18 March | The Treaty of Riga ends the war with Poland. Some historians use this date as an end to the Civil War, although fighting continues |
| 1921 | April | Severe famine begins in the Volga region |
| 1922 | February | The *Cheka* (the secret police) is reorganised and becomes the GPU (State Political Administration) |
| 1922 | March–April | Stalin is elected to the position of General Secretary of the Communist Party at the 11th Party Congress. Lenin is recovering from an operation to remove the two bullets from the assassination attempt of 1918 |
| 1922 | April | House arrest of Patriarch Tikhon of the Russian Orthodox Church |

*Source 1*

'The execution of the Tsar's family was needed not only to frighten, horrify and instil a sense of hopelessness in the enemy, but also to shake up our own ranks, to show that there was no retreating, that ahead lay either total victory or total doom.'

**Leon Trotsky, *Diary*, 9 April 1935**

Trotsky wrote this over 15 years *after* the decision was made to kill the Tsar. Some historians believe that the Tsar and his family were shot because the Czech Legion was close enough to plan a rescue attempt.

1 Would you trust the reason given here to be accurate? Be prepared to justify any comments you might make or reservations that you have!

2 Does it matter when, or where, accounts of the past are recorded by eye-witness participants?

*Source 2*

'Their [Czech Legion] success was a death sentence for Nicholas and his family. The Party did not want to give the Whites any live banner to rally round . They had begun to murder every Romanov they could find, starting with Grand Duke Mikhail on the night of June 12th. By mid-July the Czechs had outflanked Yekaterinburg ...The Romanovs died, with their children and their pets, as in gangster massacres.'

**Brian Moynahan, *The Russian Century*, 1994**

3 Do Sources 1 and 2 agree as to the Bolshevik motive for the execution of the Royal family?

4 Is there any evidence in Source 2 of a subjective approach by the author?

# Interpreting the Civil War

Under Communist rule, Western historians were denied access to many records, especially any that portrayed the Soviets in a poor light, and Western historians agreed that they would be unable fully to account for controversial events such as the Civil War:

> 'For historians of Russia interested in the twentieth century it was until recently traditional to include ... a disclaimer about the problems caused by the closure of the Soviet archives ... thus ... as late as 1990 Bruce Lincoln could bemoan in his *Red Victory* (Simon and Schuster, 1990) that parts of Russia's Civil War Story will almost certainly never be told for the documents remain locked away in the Soviet archives '
>
> **V. P. Butt, A. B. Murphy, N. A. Myshov and G. Swain, The Russian Civil War: Documents from the Soviet Archives, 1996**

## RE-INTERPRETING THE PAST

However, these writers felt that Western and Soviet historians were reaching similar conclusions about the Civil War, although newly released documents suggest that the debate has been oversimplified:

> 'Events of 1918–22 reflected struggles and tensions in Russian society far more complex than the simple Red–White struggle of "progress" versus "reaction", and foreshadow all the horrors of the Stalin period. They remind us first that many of the Whites were not "White" at all, and that the Civil War began as a war between the Bolsheviks and their socialist opponents – the ... Socialist Revolutionaries. They [documents] show a regime founded on terror, and which relied on terror throughout the war. They show that while the Red Army was able to defeat the Whites, it was not the disciplined army of Bolshevik propaganda. Desertion, low morale and poor supplies dogged it at every level; and the much vaunted commissar system of political education scarcely operated.'

The earlier opinion, that the Red Army eventually triumphed by being better organised and motivated than their opponents, by having natural advantages – they were in the central, key regions of the Russian Empire – and by pursuing the policy of War Communism may have to be re-examined.

## THE IMPACT OF THE CIVIL WAR

The Civil War was a key time in forming the attitudes and polices of many of the Soviet leadership. The struggle to win was absolute. Either sacrifices had to be made or the revolution would fail. Some historians argue that this internal conflict, with so many outside participants, was to push Russia towards the dictatorship of one party and eventually the dictatorship of one leader:

> 'Only by placing all human and natural resources within reach and at the service of a government that spoke in the name of the people but acted in the interests of the Communist Party did Lenin and his comrades defeat their enemies.'
>
> **Bruce Lincoln, Red Victory, 1990**

Of course, this was not presented in this way to the Soviet people. The Civil War was a heroic struggle against the forces of oppression that sought to overthrow the people's state. For example, the food shortages of the postwar years were reported as food hoarding, despite there being enough for everyone, by selfish individuals in the hope of making massive profits:

---

## THE KEY ISSUE

Looking at differing interpretations in historical writing

## THE KEY SKILLS

Analysis and evaluation
Assessment: historiography and the nature of sources

## WHAT YOU HAVE TO DO

Look at the events of the Civil War, and the issues of cause and consequence, principally deciding why the Bolsheviks won, and the nature and influence of Trotsky's tactics.

### Why did the Bolsheviks win?

Trotsky is usually credited with having played a major role in reforming the Bolshevik military machine and in the Bolshevik victory in the Civil War.

### What were Trotsky's tactics?

- Raising of morale and confidence
- Re-introduction of capital punishment for soldiers
- Promotion of able soldiers
- Introduction of conscription

You could consider What Happened in the Civil War, and ask Why did the Bolsheviks Win? Or you could ask What was the Impact of the Civil War on Russia's Land, Economy, and People?

'No one can eat more than the body can absorb. Everyone is provided for. And yet there is concealment everywhere, in the hope of selling ... to speculators at fabulous prices.'

*Bolshevik report, 1919*

Propaganda worked overtime to colour every event and to portray even the most bitter disaster as a victory for idealism and eventual victory.

Was the Civil War solely for the benefit of the Communist Party, or were wider issues at stake? Certainly there is documentary evidence to show that the Soviet leadership were having difficulties agreeing how best to pursue the war:

'As hopes of a European revolution waned, and the regime became embroiled in the frantic struggle to defeat the whites and their foreign backers, arguments erupted over strategy and tactics.'

*Chris Ward, Stalin's Russia, 1993*

## EVENTS: 1922–1924

| | | |
|---|---|---|
| 1922 | 16 April | The Treaty of Rapallo with Germany agrees close economic ties and military co-operation, and the Soviet leadership hope that it will herald their return to the international community |
| 1922 | 26 May | Lenin has a first stroke. A second in December weakens him further and on 23–26 December he dictates his 'Letter to the Congress' or *Testament* (will), stating his plans for the future. Lenin and Stalin have major policy disagreements, Lenin criticises Stalin for being overly brutal. He adds a codicil to his letter on 4 January 1923, warning against Stalin's power and character |
| 1923 | April | 12th Party Congress |
| 1923 | 30 December | Russia adopts the title USSR (Union of Soviet Socialist Republics, or CCCP in Russian) and forms a federation consisting of Russia, Transcaucasia, White Russia and the Ukraine |
| 1923 | March | Lenin's third stroke |
| 1923 | July | Constitution of the USSR published |
| 1924 | 21 January | Lenin dies. His *Testament* is read out to the Politburo. No action is taken against Stalin, as many see him as useful in holding back Trotsky's power |
| 1924 | 1 February | Great Britain recognises the Soviet regime |

*A scene from the famine during the Civil War*

White forces – forces that were anti-Bolshevik: this includes a rainbow alliance, that never worked effectively or in close co-operation

Czech Legion – originally an army helping the Russians against the Austrians/Germans, they turned against the Bolsheviks in order to protect the new state of Czechoslovakia

See the following general texts: Chapter 7, Section 3 of Michael Lynch, *Reaction and Revolutions: 1881–1924* (Hodder and Stoughton (1992); and Chapter 3 of Geoffrey Hosking, *A History of the Soviet Union 1917–1991* (Fontana, 1992 edn). Or you could look at these original sources: V. P. Butt, A. B. Murphy, N. A. Myshov and G. Swain (eds), *The Russian Civil War: Documents from the Soviet Archives* (Macmillan, 1996); or The Library of Congress Internet site on *Russian History*.

### The cost of the Civil War

An estimated 10 million Russians died – half due to famine. Industry was dedicated to war production and output fell dramatically. The *Cheka* became even more feared: many Russians were arrested without being guilty of crimes. Vast areas were disrupted by fighting and there was considerable social dislocation. The Bolsheviks became immensely unpopular and had to rule by terror rather than consensus.

## THE KEY ISSUES

- What were the policies of Lenin's government and how did they change Russia?
- Why was there a power struggle after Lenin's death in 1924?
- Who were the key figures of post-Leninist Russia?
- How do politicians use propaganda to create a larger-than-life image?
- What should we do to evaluate propaganda and iconographic evidence?

## THE KEY SKILLS

Interpretation: personalities in history
Research: biographical detail and events
Evaluation
Communication

## WHAT YOU HAVE TO DO

Think about why some individuals are able to triumph over others. Research the details of the power struggle that led to Stalin's rise and Trotsky's death.

**Thinking about propaganda and image**

Before you begin:
- What are the requirements of successful propaganda?
- How might propaganda be different during peacetime and wartime?

To what extent, and at what cost, did Lenin succeed in making Russia a successful Communist state from 1918 to 1924? **?**

# Lenin's Achievements

## THE ROLE OF PERSONALITIES IN HISTORY

There is a danger in Russian history of focusing on the lives and contributions of a small number of men – principally the Tsars, Kerensky, Lenin, Trotsky and Stalin. These figures typify the periods that they represent and bear much of the responsibility for the actions and events of the governments that they led. Historians have traditionally based their studies around these men, and this has shaped the end result – the histories. Here we do the same: we present a picture of the main themes of the age, and the main figures who led and shaped the age. Remember that historical work is in progress that examines the roles of others in history – the ordinary man and woman – and the part that local history has to play in reconstructing the past.

### LENIN THE HERO?

This picture of Lenin in classic pose is one of the most recognisable of the 20th century, but what makes it an effective image? Lenin has became almost a trademark – a brand image. The founder of the world's first Communist state has, by the success of his own propaganda, been reduced to an icon.

*Vladimir Lenin, Russian revolutionary*

### POLICY AND PROGRESS

By 1921, the Russian economy had been devastated by the Civil War and the policy of War Communism. Industrial production and grain harvests were low and black-marketeering flourished. The drought of 1921 caused widespread famine and Russia required international aid to avert total collapse. Even so, as many as 5 million died. Despite the *Cheka* there were rumblings of discontent. Protest was led by supporters of Bolshevism as well as by opponents. The Commissar for Social Welfare, Alexandra Mikhailovna Kollontai, agitated for reform, and relief of suffering. Her extreme (by the standards of the time) feminism meant that she was sidelined into becoming a diplomat, and she became the world's first female ambassador.

In March 1921, the Naval Base at Kronstadt (Petrograd) mutinied. This base had always been a fervent supporter of the Bolsheviks – which shows the strength of feeling – and Trotsky was sent to crush the opposition. As a result, 20 000 were killed as a result and thousands were imprisoned or executed. The outcome of the revolt was a change of policy. Lenin issued the New Economic Policy, which was effectively a watering down of Communism, to provide a 'breathing space' for the country,. It said that small companies could be privately owned and run; targets for food production were set, but forced confiscation of crops was halted (once targets had been met, any surplus belonged to the producer); private trade and profit were allowed; and sales of some surpluses from state concerns were allowed.

As a result, agricultural production increased and foreign investors reconsidered links with Lenin's Russia. Many Communists were uneasy with this policy. Historians disagree about the reliability of Russian figures regarding production, but agree that the NEP seems to have calmed things down in Russia. Keeping the people content meant raising their living standards without a trade deficit. Lenin encouraged small-scale industrialisation, and a major programme of electrification was initiated. The slogan 'Soviet Power Plus Electrification Equals Communism' was circulated across the Soviet Union.

## Hearts and Minds – Policies to Shape Attitudes

The promise of better times ahead is a powerful incentive, provided that better times do eventually arrive. The Communist Party had to ensure that the workers and party officials believed not only that the promises made could be delivered, but that they were being delivered somewhere in the Soviet Union. The purpose of Soviet propaganda was to win hearts and shape minds, and a distinctive school of propaganda art developed, building on influences in European art of the period.

The availability of education before the Revolution was patchy, and the Communists invested heavily to raise standards. Literacy schemes for adults were launched, further and higher education were expanded, and the *Komsomol*, a youth organisation, took care of political education of the young.

## Relationships and the Family

Ranks and titles were abolished. The Commissar for Social Welfare, Alexandra Kollontai, arranged for easier marriage and divorce and advocated freedom to be with any sexual partner of choice. Collective child-care centres (kindergartens) were set up. Abortion was to be available on demand. Women were encouraged to break away from their traditional role in the home, and to work outside the family unit. These policies met with varied success, and although conservatives were outraged at the imagined impact, little changed except for an improved regard for women in the workplace.

## Religion

Marx had said that 'Religion is the opiate of the people', meaning that it was a tool to oppress and keep people obedient to the established order.

- *Christianity*. The pre-revolutionary Russian Orthodox Church was wealthy and influential. Much of its leadership had sided with the Whites in the Civil War, and relations between the Communists and the church were poor. Church land was confiscated, priests were arrested or exiled, and the church was forbidden to teach young people. Priests were given higher taxes and lower rations, and their children were denied higher education.
- *Islam*. Although the Bolsheviks initially did not interfere with the Islamic Church, as the Communist grasp on the southern and eastern republics increased, Muslim schools, mosques and hospitals were closed, and teaching of Islam outside of the family was forbidden.
- *Judaism*. Pogroms and anti-Semitic policies are features of Russian history, with Jewish citizens treated with as much disregard as other 'believers'. Stalinist propaganda emphasised that Trotsky came from a Jewish background, and anti-Semitic images on some posters were not uncommon.

Your subtitles could follow some of those used on pages 28 and 29.

## Who were the key figures of post-Leninist Russia?

'If Stalin were an ambitious man so were all the other contenders for power. If Stalin changed his mind on key issues of the day, so did the others.'
**Chris Ward, *Stalin's Russia*, 1993**

Traditionally, historians have looked at the power struggle between Trotsky and Stalin, but of course other key figures in the inner circle of Communist leaders were involved.

Research and write a short biography of the 1924 Politburo members: Trotsky (Commissar for War); Stalin (Secretary of the Communist Party); Kamenev (Politburo Chairman); Rykov (Chairman of Sovnarkom); Zinoviev (Chairman of Comintern); Bukharin (Propaganda) and Tomsky (Trade Union Affairs).

*Include* dates of birth (year) and death; key issues in the person's background and education; posts and responsibilities held within the Soviet system; and comments about their final years and death.

When you look up one person in a biographical dictionary or reference book, links are often shown to other related persons (usually in *italics*).

## THE KEY ISSUES

- Narrative: What were the events of the power struggle? Who won and why?
- Analysis: Was Trotsky a better revolutionary than Stalin? Why was Stalin a more successful politician than Trotsky?
- Historiography: What have historians said about both men and the impact of their rivalry?

## THE KEY SKILLS

Research and selection
Analysis
Synthesis

## WHAT YOU HAVE TO DO

Find out more about the relationship between Trotsky and Stalin. This will lay the foundations for later work and is a useful introduction to Stalin's later actions and attitudes. Trotsky was a brilliant thinker. Stalin was a brilliant schemer. It is important to investigate the details of the power struggle, and look at the characters of both men in more detail.

*Josef Stalin*

*Leon Trotsky*

# Lenin's Legacy: Power Struggles, 1924–1928

On his death, the Russian people seem to have been devastated by the loss of their leader. Reports released by the authorities cite thousands of distraught mourners filing past Lenin's body as it lay in state, and hundreds of thousands more visitors viewed Lenin in his mausoleum. How did the Soviet leadership appoint a successor to Lenin?

## WHO IS THE HEIR?

The Politburo of Bukharin, Kamenev, Rykov, Stalin, Tomsky, Trotsky and Zinoviev initially agreed to share power. But during the 1930s Stalin removed each of his former colleagues. The background to this is that as Lenin approached the end of his life key figures began to consider his successor. Was there a natural heir? Although Trotsky had shown great ability in ensuring success in difficult circumstances, he was seen as arrogant by several Politburo colleagues. Stalin was General Secretary of the party, and could appoint people to posts and control membership. In the early 1920s he expelled a number of people, possibly mostly supporters of Trotsky's ideas, from the party because of their 'wild' beliefs.

## JOSEF STALIN, ORIGINALLY DZHUGASHVILI (1879–1953)

> 'He's not an intellectual like the other people you will meet ... but he knows what he wants. He's got willpower, and he's going to be top of the pile some day.'
>
> ***John Reed, Ten Days that Shook the World, 1919***

The son of a cobbler, he was born in Georgia, and educated at Tiflis Theological College, until he was expelled in 1899 for his revolutionary ideas. He was exiled to Siberia by the Tsarist authorities in 1902 and 1913. He was a leading Bolshevik in the revolutions of 1917, and became Commissar for Nationalities in their first government. He was also a member of the Politburo. Elected to the post of First Secretary to the Communist Party in 1922, he edged opponents out of his way after Lenin's death in 1924, and purged the party of opponents, becoming sole leader and virtual dictator until his death in 1953.

## LEON TROTSKY, ORIGINALLY LEV DAVIDOVICH BRONSTEIN (1879–1940)

A brilliant politician from a Jewish family, he was educated in Odessa, and spent much of his early life engaging in revolutionary activities. He was exiled to Siberia in 1898. He returned, was involved in the failed 1905 Revolution, and during 1917 was a leading member of the Bolshevik Party and became Commissar for Foreign Affairs (1917–1918) and Commissar for War (1918–1920). In 1924 Trotsky was quickly undermined by Stalin and was expelled from party membership in 1927, then exiled to central Asia, and expelled from the USSR in 1929. His continued criticism of the Soviet leaders led to an accusation of attempting the overthrow of the Soviet state, and a death sentence was passed on him in his absence. He was assassinated by a Soviet agent, who beat him to death with an ice pick in Mexico.

## WHAT DID LENIN THINK OF STALIN?

Lenin seems to have become worried about Stalin's tactics, described as too brutal and self-serving. Lenin suggested that Stalin be removed from office and replaced with someone less ambitious. The leadership disliked Trotsky, and did not want Lenin's other comments – which included criticisms of them – to be made public, and so ignored Lenin's advice. Trotsky was unwell, and Stalin persuaded him to stay away from Lenin's funeral, and so it became possible to suggest that Trotsky did not respect Lenin, and that he had deliberately stayed away from the funeral.

## STALIN VICTORIOUS

Stalin set about having Trotsky distanced from decision-making and policy discussion, by filling jobs with his supporters, and edged Trotsky out of office. Stalin also removed his previous supporters: Zinoviev and Kamenev were removed from the Politburo in 1926. By 1929 Stalin was confident enough to have Bukharin and the right-wingers removed, leaving him as undisputed leader. Further steps were taken to remove threats or any whose loyalty was in doubt during the purges of the 1930s (see Chapter 6).

## EVENTS: 1924–1940

The power struggle

| | | |
|---|---|---|
| 1924 | 23 May | 13th Party Congress; Zinoviev attacks Trotsky's ideas |
| 1925 | 16 January | By careful manoeuvring, Stalin forces Trotsky to resign as Commissar for War |
| 1925 | April | 14th Party Congress accepts principle of 'Socialism in one country' |
| 1926 | 19 October | Trotsky and Kamenev expelled from the Politburo |
| 1927 | 26 May | Great Britain suspends diplomatic relations with the USSR over arguments about Soviet propaganda |
| 1927 | November | Trotsky's supporters demonstrate and Trotsky is expelled from the Communist Party in punishment |
| 1927 | December | 15th Party Congress forbids discussion or deviation from official policy by Politburo members. Increasingly, Stalin acts against those who disagree with his views. The Conference agrees to introduce farming reforms, including the collectivisation of farms |
| 1929 | | Trotsky is expelled from the USSR, moving to France, then Oslo, and in 1937 to Mexico. During his exile he continues to write articles critical of Stalin |
| 1940 | 20 August | Trotsky is assassinated by Ramon Mercader, a hit man hired by Soviet agents. Autopsy shows a brain of 'extraordinary dimension' |

## FOLLOWING IN LENIN'S FOOTSTEPS?

Although he resisted being presented as an icon, Lenin realised that propaganda was a useful tool, after terror, in the Bolshevik armoury. Bolshevik propaganda used personalities as heroic figures and presented the leadership as almost mythical heroes, and hence can reveal much about the nature of the Soviet leadership and society.

Soviet propaganda worked hard to idolise Lenin and create a personality cult around him. Lenin, 'Hero of the Revolution', became a benchmark against which others could measure themselves. Were things being done in the way Lenin would have wanted? Would Lenin have approved of policies? Certainly questions such as these allowed Stalin to establish an orthodoxy based on what he thought was best.

### Evaluating the evidence

You do not have to doubt every source, but you should exercise *critical awareness*. Look at the origin and content of the source. When was it created and by whom? Is the originator likely to have been well informed?

Are they reporting the facts fairly and objectively? Is there any other motive in recording this evidence?

## Using photographic evidence

Look at the photograph on this page.
- What is happening?
- What might suggest that this is a propaganda photograph?

Are posed and propaganda photographs of limited value to the historian?

# Using Statistics in History: the Five Year Plans

Stalin knew that the USSR needed to industrialise. With little modern industry and vulnerable to fluctuations in the world economy, the USSR was desperately short of foreign currency for international trade. In order to develop industries, to produce armaments and agricultural equipment, a series of Five Year Plans were introduced. State planning would overcome obstacles, so there should be no delays or difficulties: any serious failure to meet targets was attributed to deliberate opposition and sabotage. The first plan, for 1928–1932, concentrated on heavy industries – coal, iron and steel, oil and electricity – and great progress was made towards unreasonably high targets. The 1933–1937 plan re-emphasised heavy industries and included communications and chemical works.

## THE FIVE YEAR PLAN FOR AGRICULTURE

First set out in 1929, this is the most notorious of the Five Year Plans. It introduced collectivisation of farming, which meant that the peasant farmers who owned a little land and grew private crops and animals were to put them

The banner reads 'We demand collectivisation and the wiping out of all Kulaks'

together, and make larger, state-run collectives. To ensure that the initial resistance to this scheme by the wealthier peasant farmer – the *kulak* – was not repeated, Stalin's secret police arrested and executed thousands of rural farmers and their families. To put the plan into effect, huge changes were required in agriculture, and this was only achieved with enormous hardship and loss of life:

'We must smash the Kulaks ... we must strike at the Kulaks so hard as to prevent them rising to their feet again. We must destroy them as a social class.'
**Josef Stalin, at the 1929 Party Conference**

## USING STATISTICS TO EXAMINE THE FIVE YEAR PLANS

A series of statistical sources, all based on Soviet figures for the period of the Five Year Plans for Agriculture, are presented here. Look carefully and decide what they might tell you about the Russian economy and society under Stalin.

*Source 1*
The population of the Soviet Union (millions):

| | |
|---|---|
| 1914 | 140.4 (estimate) |
| 1926 | 147.0 |
| 1939 | 170.5 |
| 1940 | 194.1 (includes newly annexed territories) |
| 1950 | 178.5 |
| 1959 | 208.8 |

*From G. Hosking, A History of the Soviet Union, 1992, quoting Soviet statistics*

## Source 2

The social classes within Soviet society (millions):

| Year | Workers | Individual peasants | Collective peasants | White collar | Bourgeoisie and landowners |
|------|---------|--------------------|--------------------|-------------|---------------------------|
| 1913 | 14.6 | 66.7 | – | 2.4 | 16.3 |
| 1924 | 10.4 | 75.4 | 1.3 | 4.4 | 8.5 |
| 1928 | 12.4 | 74.9 | 2.9 | 5.2 | 4.6 |
| 1939 | 33.7 | 2.6 | 47.2 | 16.5 | |
| 1959 | 50.2 | 0.3 | 31.4 | 18.1 | |

*From G. Hosking, A History of the Soviet Union, 1992, quoting Soviet statistics*

## Source 3

Selected production indices:

| | 1913 | 1922 | 1928 | 1932 | 1940 | 1945 | 1950 | 1960 |
|---|------|------|------|------|------|------|------|------|
| Steel (m tonnes) | 4.3 | 0.3 | 4.0 | 5.9 | 18.3 | 12.3 | 27.3 | 65.3 |
| Coal (m tonnes) | 29.2 | 11.3 | 35.4 | 64.3 | 165.9 | 149.3 | 261.1 | 510 |
| Oil (m tonnes) | 10.3 | 4.7 | 11.7 | 21.4 | 31.1 | 19.4 | 37.9 | 148 |
| Electricity (10⁹ kWh) | 2.0 | 0.8 | 5.1 | 13.4 | 48.6 | 43.2 | 91.2 | 292 |
| Automobiles (thousands) | | | 0.8 | | 145 | 74.7 | 363 | 524 |
| Tractors (thousands) | | | 1.3 | 48.9 | 31.6 | 14.7 | 109 | 239 |
| Wool (cloth, m metres) | 107.7 | 37 | 97 | 93.3 | 119.7 | 53.6 | 155.2 | 439 |
| Leather footwear (m pairs) | 60 | 6.8 | 58 | 86.9 | 211 | 63 | 203 | 419 |
| Grain (m tonnes) | 76.5 | 50.3 | 73.3 | 69.6 | 95.6 | 47.3 | 81.2 | 126 |
| Meat (m tonnes) | | 2.2 | | | 4.7 | | | 8.7 |
| Milk (m tonnes) | | 24.5 | | | 33.6 | | | 67.1 |
| Sugar (m tonnes) | 1.3 | 0.2 | 1.3 | 0.8 | 2.2 | 0.5 | 2.5 | 6.4 |
| Cows (m head) | 24.9 | | 29.3 | 22.3 | 22.8 | 22.9 | 24.6 | 34.8 |
| Pigs (m head) | 17.3 | | 22.0 | 10.9 | 22.5 | 10.6 | 22.2 | 58.7 |

*From G. Hosking, A History of the Soviet Union, 1992, quoting Soviet statistics (Hosking notes that they may be incorrect, but might show some valuable points)*

## Source 4

The percentage of peasant households collectivised:

| 1930 | 23.6% |
|------|-------|
| 1931 | 52.7% |
| 1932 | 61.5% |
| 1933 | 64.4% |
| 1934 | 71.4% |
| 1935 | 83.2% |
| 1936 | 89.9% |

## Source 5

The percentage of crop area collectivised:

| 1930 | 33.6% |
|------|-------|
| 1931 | 67.8% |
| 1932 | 76.6% |
| 1933 | 83.1% |
| 1934 | 87.4% |
| 1935 | 94.1% |
| 1936 | No figures |

*From Sotsialisticheskoe strooitel'stvo SSSR (1936), quoted in Alec Nove, An Economic History of the USSR, 1992*

## Source 6

State grain procurements (millions of tons):

| 1928 | 10.8 |
|------|------|
| 1929 | 16.1 |
| 1930 | 22.1 |
| 1931 | 22.8 |
| 1932 | 18.5 |
| 1933 | 22.6 |

## Source 7

Grain exports (millions of tons):

| 1927–1928 | 0.029 |
|-----------|-------|
| 1929 | 0.18 |
| 1930 | 4.76 |
| 1931 | 5.06 |
| 1932 | 1.76 |
| 1933 | 1.69 |

*From Alec Nove, An Economic History of the USSR, 1992, quoting Soviet trade reports and official archives*

## INTERPRETING STATISTICS

The statistics provide the basis for analysis, but they are 'raw' statistics. They have been drawn together from a variety of 'official' Soviet statistics, and reflect the picture that the Communist state was prepared to release. Statistics presented as figures may well be 'safer' than those presented as graphs and diagrams. The artist has to decide on scale and design, and graphs are open to abuse depending on the scales used and the size of units presented. Look at the rates of growth or decline. Are the units even? Are the scales deceptive? What is the origin of the figures? Of course you can have perfectly honest figures – make sure that you explain and support any assertions that you make based on statistics.

### Using statistics in history

When using official statistics or documents, there is a temptation to trust the material blindly. But in fact there are often very good reasons why a government will distort and carefully edit the truth. It is not always in everyone's interest to know everything that is true!

'There are two kinds of statistics – the kind that you look up, and the kind that you make up.'

**Rex Stout, author**

### Working on the case study

Look at the statistics provided here. Use the figures of your choice to support the view that collectivisation was proving to be successful. Set yourself a time limit and then present your findings as either a report, a seminar or to others in your study group. You might compare figures that reveal that various indicators were showing progress, compare early figures with later ones, or construct a general argument that draws on individual examples to construct a case. Working in pairs will allow you to share ideas and develop a joint interpretation.

1 What uses can information and communication technology bring to the study of history?

2 What do we mean by the term 'statistics'? What are the drawbacks of statistical data for the historian?

## THE KEY ISSUES

- What were the published results of the first Five Year Plan?
- In what areas of the economy did Stalin claim the USSR was making rapid progress? Can we trust the claims made?
- What did Stalin do as a result of the statistics he was receiving?

## THE KEY SKILLS

Using and interpreting statistics
Assessing value, reliability and influences on evidence

## WHAT YOU HAVE TO DO

Think about how and why Stalin's policies and reactions were beginning to distort the historical record in the USSR by the 1930s.

'You cannot feed the hungry on statistics.'

**David Lloyd George, British politician**

### Re-evaluating the statistics

Use any of the statistics and any other historical argument that you can devise to challenge or disprove the theory that statistics proved that collectivisation was working. Questions that might help are as follows:

- Are the statistics accurate? If, not, where and why might inaccuracy occur?
- How could we verify the figures?
- What is the significance of the fact that figures might not be correct, and are they still of value if they are distorted?

Remember that historical debate still centres on the accuracy of the available figures, particularly as new archives are opening up all the time.

# *Success or Failure?*

## ARE SOVIET STATISTICS ACCURATE?

Historians have a healthy respect for facts, but what constitutes a fact? There are very few 'facts' in history at all. History is a fragmentary and incomplete record, and we often have only a poor representation of the past.

There can be a tendency to doubt the human evidence of the past, such as letters or diaries, and yet accept the more 'scientific' evidence, such as photographs or official figures. Photographs can be manipulated, but what of statistics? Historians agree that the industrialisation of the Soviet Union was a remarkable feat, but to what extent can we trust the actual figures?

There is considerable scope for inaccuracy within the figures as presented here and elsewhere. All Stalinist statistics (especially of national income and industrial production) are possibly inflated by human action, and because the way in which the statistics were measured allowed inaccuracy. Officials had to meet targets or suffer, and so the figures often said that targets were met even when the reality of stock in warehouses differed. Data collection on the scale attempted under the secretive Soviet state encouraged inaccuracy, and so we often doubt the true level of improvements achieved.

## LOOKING AT THE FIRST FIVE YEAR PLAN

What, then, were the results of the 'Great Leap Forwards'? There was a claimed over-production of machinery and construction (although metal and fuel outputs were well below planned levels); small production businesses were deliberately squeezed, and skilled craftsmen appear to have been forced into larger collectives.

New towns were set up to develop specific industries close to the source of raw materials, and there was a population shift from rural communities to the new urban centres. This move from urbanisation (according to Alec Nove) pushed standards of living down, because although output increased individual welfare decreased, and standards of living remained virtually static. Housing, transport, water, food and public health facilities were at breaking point. The plan allowed for 6.3 square metres of living space per person in housing, but failed to achieve its target and housing was much more cramped.

Inflation, taxes and prices rose. Purchasing power and the availability of a number of goods fell. State control over the availability of some goods was tightened, effectively rationing some essential items.

*Source 8*
Law of 7 April 1932:
Penalty for the pilfering of foodstuffs in *kolkhozes* (collective farms): death

*Source 9*
Official fixed prices and black market prices (in kopeks per kilogram):

| | Private market prices | | | | | Official price | Free market price |
|---|---|---|---|---|---|---|---|
| | 1928 | 1929 | 1930 | 1931 | 1932 | | |
| Rye flour | 100 | 225 | 350 | 525 | 2303 | 12.6 | 89.5 |
| Potatoes | 100 | 160 | 280 | 520 | 1552 | | |
| Beef | 100 | 125 | 359 | 663 | 1264 | 111 | 414 |
| Butter | 100 | 201 | 602 | 979 | 1078 | 502 | 1146 |
| Eggs | 100 | 134 | 330 | 572 | 868 | | |
| Rye bread | — | — | — | — | — | 10.5 | 111.0 |

*From Alec Nove, quoting Soviet statistics*

Source 10

Housing construction (million square metres):

|  | |
|---|---|
| 1918–1928 | 203 |
| 1929–1932 (1st FYP) | 203 |
| 1933–1937 (2nd FYP) | 56.9 |
| 1937–June 1941 (3rd FYP) | 81.7 |
| July 1941–1945 | 102.5 |
| 1946–1950 (4th FYP) | 200.9 |
| 1951–1955 (5th FYP) | 240.5 |

*From G. Hosking, A History of the Soviet Union, 1992,*
*quoting Narodnoe Khozyaistvo SSSR, 1922–87*

## WAS STALIN SATISFIED?

During the late 1920s and early 1930s, many senior state farm officials, industrialists, scientists and engineers were arrested and put on public or show trial. Many were shot, while others were exiled to remote parts of the USSR, or were given long prison sentences. Most charges were based on accusations of sabotage, alleged spying, wrecking the economy or causing food shortages. Despite this, Stalin seems to have felt that good progress was being made, and genuinely believed that any failure was down to anti-social elements. His bitter war against the *kulaks* was based on a conviction that it was the only way to progress on a massive scale. He believed that the USSR must make the Great Leap Forwards or fail.

Stalin seems to have been dominated by threats from within Russia and by a belief that he could not trust the international community. Even relations with socialist governments were often strained. In a sense, he was proved right. Preparing the USSR to compete with the world also prepared it for the war in 1941, and despite misinterpreting Hitler's intentions Russia was in a much stronger position as a result of the Five Year Plans. Economic and industrial planning in the 1930s reflect Soviet anticipation of a war with Germany, although the positioning of some enterprises shows that Stalin never anticipated losing so much land early in the war. Evacuation of materials and plant was carried out on an incredible scale, but much fell to the German *Blitzkrieg*. Completion of the Third Five Year Plan was interrupted by the Great Fatherland War, and the USSR suffered unprecedented loss of life, infrastructure and property.

Even after much progress by 1945, after the first two plans, Stalin wrote 'We are fifty or a hundred years behind the advanced countries. We must make good this distance in ten years. Either we do it or we go under.'

## INTERPRETING THE FIVE YEAR PLANS

Committing the Soviet Union to the Five Year Plans undoubtedly resulted in a stronger and more self-sufficient economy, and historians are able to see the benefits that the plans brought. Historical debate centres on whether the limitations of the Soviet economy justified the harsh methods and terror tactics; the extent to which difficulties with economic policy and targets helped foster Stalin's personal paranoia and the purges; and the extent to which Stalin genuinely believed that an international conspiracy existed to destroy the Soviet Union, and thus that they had to progress or fail.

Stalin had no choice but to present his economic policies and their results to the Soviet Union, and to the hostile world, as a great success. Central economic planning was inextricably linked to the Communist state, and all later Communist states seem to have been willing to believe that they will succeed where Stalin failed. Now that there is freer access to archives and oral evidence, much work remains to look at trends and statistics, and to unearth the real achievement and cost levels of the 'Great Leap Forwards'.

Do you agree that 'the ends justified the means' within Stalin's economic policies of the 1930s?

*collectivisation* – taking over small private farms to create larger, 'more efficient' collective farms: under Stalin's plans, 25 million small farms were to be made into 240 000 larger farms

*kulaks* – peasants with private land, and hence marginally wealthier: they resented the move from landowner to unpaid worker

### How will the Five Year Plans be remembered?

'The Party claimed in the Spring of 1930 that half of all peasant households had been collectivised. The effects were ruinous. A quarter of all the cattle, sheep, and goats, and a third of the pigs in the Soviet Union were slaughtered in 1930. The great bulk of them were killed and eaten in February and March by peasants who were determined that they should not be given to the collectives. The most productive peasants were herded off as Kulaks; the wastrels and idlers who denounced them flourished; the surviving middle peasants, cowed and sullen, were in no mood to exert themselves for the State.'
**Brian Moynahan, The Russian Century, 1994**

The American author Mark Twain wrote 'There are three kinds of lies – lies, damned lies and statistics'. To what extent do you agree that statistics are of no use to an historian?

## THE KEY ISSUES

- How did Stalin manipulate and control the Communist hierarchy?
- Why is the Kirov murder an important turning point?
- Did anyone resist Stalin?
- Was dictatorship inevitable?

## THE KEY SKILLS

Research
Interpretation and evaluation
Assessment: cause and consequence

## WHAT YOU HAVE TO DO

Your task here is to look at how the machinery of the secret police, the courts, the law and the labour camps were used to purge Soviet society of any potential opposition to Stalin.

'Men are too complicated, too spiritual, too various, for scientific analysis; and the life history of millions cannot be inferred from the history of single men. History, in fact, is more a matter of rough guessing from all the available facts.'

**A. L. Rowse, historian**

To what extent do you agree that the study of single individuals such as Josef Stalin can inform us about whole countries in the past?

As you read through the sections that describe Stalin's era, try to develop your own impression of Stalin. A useful source is Leon Trotsky's *The Revolution Betrayed* (Pathfinder Press, 1977; first published 1937).

# The Great Terror

## HOW DID STALIN MANIPULATE AND CONTROL THE COMMUNIST HIERARCHY?

Stalin appointed loyal supporters to vacant posts or, where necessar created vacancies to promote his underlings. He could then demand the unquestioning support; without it they were quickly removed. Initially, on Trotskyites were at risk, but then Stalin purged the inner circles of the Sovi leadership, using the secret police against senior party and state officials. this climate of fear it was necessary to show absolute loyalty to Stalin or fac the consequences. Isolation and fear proved to be powerful weapons.

In 1932 a senior official called Ryutin circulated a document whic heavily criticised Stalin, the Five Year Plans and collectivisation. Ryuti called Stalin 'the evil genius of the Russian Revolution who, activated vindictiveness and a lust for power, has brought the revolution to the edg of the abyss' (quoted in *Izvestia Tsk KPSS*, No. 6, 1989). Stalin wante Ryutin executed but instead he was exiled and expelled from the part This made Stalin suspicious. How could his colleagues not support him an protect his reputation? Who could he trust if colleagues were willing to vo against him?

Sergei Kirov was a threat, as he was popular and influential. At the 17 Party Congress Stalin set up old rivals such as Bukharin and Kamenev show their 'enthusiasm' for his leadership, which they did to get back in favour. Some senior party members asked Kirov to stand against Stalin, b he refused. Stalin was quietly furious, and on 1 December 1934 Kirov w shot dead in his Leningrad Party Office. The murderer, Nikolayev, w arrested and rapidly tried in secret and executed. Kirov's death was almo certainly ordered by Stalin himself.

The official investigation blamed a Leningrad-based 'Opposition Centr and Bukharin and Kamenev were implicated and arrested. In the followin month, 40 000 citizens of Leningrad were arrested as collaborators in Kirov murder plot. In all, it is estimated that up to a million were arrested an executed, mainly in Leningrad and Moscow. The most senior figures we Kamenev and Zinoviev, who were put on public trial, confessed their 'guil were found guilty and were shot in 1936.

*An American cartoon of the 1930s*

*The cartoon satirises 'the confessions of guilt' at the Soviet show trials. It was commonly (and correctly) believed that the accused had been told that their families were under threat if they did not co-operate*

# WHAT WAS THE 'GREAT TERROR'?

talin gradually moved through every rank of Soviet society, and from 1936 urged key personnel. The leaders of Soviet society, the armed forces and ey departments were removed. Millions were sent to labour camps, into ternal exile or sentenced and executed in show trials. Many of the key gures of the Revolution were removed from office and a new leadership ursued Stalin's goals single-mindedly.

In 1937 Stalin looked at the Politburo, the security services and the ilitary. Yagoda, the Head of the Secret Police (NKVD) was arrested: ongside Bukharin, he was tried for treason and corruption and shot. In )39 the replacement leader of the NKVD, Yezhov, was accused of being a ritish agent and also shot.

## URGE VICTIMS

1928 there were 30 000 citizens in forced labour camps. By 1938, it is timated that 7 million citizens were held. From 1929 to 1939 up to 24 illion *kulaks*, 'criminals and wreckers' were placed in labour camps, but ey were not the only target of Stalin's paranoia. Between 1934 and 1953, aders of the armed forces, police officials, party officials and up to 17 illion people were arrested, deported or simply disappeared.

Despite the risks, some citizens were prepared to speak out against their wn regime and rulers. These dissidents were subject to surveillance by the athorities and the secret police, arrest, imprisonment and harsh treatment. rganised opposition was almost impossible, but small groups or cells of pposition managed to resist the worst and retained some independence of ought and action. Through the writings of later dissidents such as lexander Solzhenitsyn, we are able to get an insight into life at this time and the years after Stalin's death.

## WAS DICTATORSHIP INEVITABLE?

learly, there were excesses under the Tsarist and Bolshevik secret police, d the party structure concentrated power in the hands of a few rather than ose of the many. There are also justifications for such a power structure. e can understand – if not always support – the view that foreign powers ere suspicious of the Soviet Union, and mistrusted its leaders. We can also e the benefits of rapid and firm decision-making. It is easier to look at use and consequence than decide if human nature leads to extremes, and erhaps we should accept that nothing is inevitable in history.

## VENTS: 1930–1940

| | | |
|---|---|---|
| )30 | April | Mayakovsky commits suicide |
| )30–1931 | | Show trials are held and executions take place of those putting the state and its progress at risk |
| )34 | December | Kirov is murdered by Stalin's agents |
| )35 | September | Ranks are reintroduced into the Red Army |
| )36 | June | New family laws make divorce more difficult |
| )36 | August | Kamenev and Zinoviev are executed, and major purges take place of senior ranks of Soviet society and Soviet leaders |
| )37 | | There is a major purge of the armed forces, police and security services |
| )38 | | Stalin's 'Short Course' is published |
| )38 | March | Bukharin and others are tried and executed |
| )38 | December | The labour book for workers is introduced |
| )38–June 1941 | | Third Five Year Plan (the 'Great Fatherland War' interrupts the plan) |
| )39 | March | 18th Party Congress |
| )40 | | Two million citizens of the Baltic states are deported east; most die |

## Was Stalin an 'evil genius'?

There will be times when you will want to comment on the effect of a policy or decision and the human costs and consequences. However, you should avoid making too robust an attack on the standards and values of past times: our values are different, and we must look at events in the context of the times. Of course, this doesn't mean you have to agree with – or approve of – what was done in the past! This is what Stalin himself said:

'The state is an instrument in the hands of the ruling class for suppressing the resistance of its class enemies.'

'Personnel selection is decisive. People are our most valuable capital.'

What do you think he meant when he made these two statements?

## Bukharin's opinion of Stalin

'On his last trip abroad in 1936 Bukharin, who already knew he was doomed ... said this is a small, wicked man ... no not a man, a devil. He is something like the symbol of the party. The rank-and-file workers, the people believe him. We are probably responsible for it ourselves ... and this is why we are all crawling into his jaws knowing for sure that he will devour us. This sort of thinking paralysed Stalin's opponents.'

**David Christian, Imperial and Soviet Russia, 1986, citing M. Lewin, Political Undercurrents in Soviet Economic Debates, 1975**

## THE KEY ISSUES

- What do we mean by the term 'personality cult'?
- How did Lenin and Stalin create and maintain personality cults?
- Does propaganda and biased evidence serve any purpose for the historian?
- Are some types of evidence better than others?

## THE KEY SKILLS

Evaluation and interpretation of sources
Communication

## WHAT YOU HAVE TO DO

Your task is to become familiar with the different types of sources that you might be asked to interpret, to gain an awareness of some of their strengths and weaknesses, and to develop a critical understanding of the problems faced by the historian in reconstructing and interpreting the past.

'In free society art is not a weapon ...
Artists are not engineers of the soul.'

**J. F. Kennedy**

1  Do you agree that art can be a useful tool for the dictator?
2  In what ways does art made as propaganda tell us about the society which created such sources and prove useful for the historian?

The core issue is What Is Propaganda? You could look at Examples of Ways of Delivering Propaganda, and give Some Examples of Propaganda. Then comment on the question Does Propaganda Work?

# 'What I Tell you Three Times is True'

Adolf Hitler said that 'the great masses of the people will more easily fa victim to a big lie than a small one', and the 1930s and 1940s are a testame to dictators' skills of oratory, and the propagandist's art. Here we will look the ways in which key messages were repeated and restated to drum the home to the people.

Lenin quickly latched on to the value of propaganda and public speakin The following tools can be used to convince the public:

- *Oratory – public speaking and recorded speech via the radio and other method* Both Trotsky and Lenin were masterly speakers and could captivate a audience. Stalin had less panache, but was able to argue a convincing cas Debating in Bolshevik and in Communist Party circles or committe developed such skills, and they were put to good use. Trotsky in particul travelled great distances on a special train to speak to crowds of worke and peasants, and spoke to mass meetings.
- *Propaganda posters, slogans and photographs.* The use of visual images was powerful and important tool. As many ordinary Soviet citizens we unable to read, and there were many languages spoken, photographs ar symbols were easy to interpret and remember. Slogans were also powerf if repeated enough and displayed prominently. They were much used: f example, 'Soviet Power Plus Electrification Equals Communism'.
- *Film.* Lenin realised the power of the moving image. History could replayed, and – when the facts were inconvenient – remade! The Sovi director Sergei Eisenstein produced two great works of cinema propaganda: *Potemkin*, about the 1905 Revolution, and *October*, based the Bolshevik version of events in 1917.
- *Leaflets, polemics and treatises.* Today we see so many written items in o everyday lives that it is easy to forget that people in the past took the tir to look at new ideas and opinions, even if they disagreed with them.
- *Newspapers and magazines.* Newspapers looked very different earlier th century to the way that they look today, and although largely a town- ar city-based medium (because that is where the presses and population we based) they did have an impact on opinion and were used to good effe It is worth noting that the title of the Russian newspaper *Pravda* mea 'truth'.

## WHAT DO WE MEAN BY THE TERM 'PERSONALITY CULT?'

Historians sometimes write about historical figures and their creation of personality cult. This means that the leader deliberately created – or othe created after their death – an idealised view of the person. Their go qualities are exaggerated, and their limitations diminished. Twentiet century examples include Lenin, Stalin, Mussolini and Hitler.

Another term that you might see used is 'iconography', meaning t creation of images and objects to associate a person with certain qualities. the case of the great dictators, this often takes the form of posters ar pictures. Early Stalinist posters associate Stalin with Lenin, and Stal encouraged others to refer to him as the 'new' Lenin. Later posters gave h semi-religious qualities, with his face appearing in the middle of rays sunlight.

Khrushchev, Stalin's successor, condemned Stalin at the 20th Party Congress in 1956 by implying that Stalinist rule had flaws, and that many errors had occurred because Stalin did not rule in the USSR's interests. The leadership under Khrushchev were largely the people who had supported Stalin, and their joint blame and guilt seems to have been conveniently forgotten. Stalin's 'crimes' were attributed to his personally going astray rather than to the system being in error.

## WHY WAS PROPAGANDA NECESSARY?

The Soviet Union was a massive state, and millions of its citizens would only ever see their leaders portraits on stamps and coins, and learn of their policies through controlled state-run press and media. Unlike any earlier nation, Bolshevik Russia developed the art of propaganda. The slogan, the poster and the speech preceded policy. For people whose first language was not Russian, whose literacy levels were not high, or for whom politics and economics were remote concepts, propaganda was the key to winning ideas, minds and souls.

In the short term, the Soviet authorities could cajole their peoples into even greater efforts and sacrifices for the state, but what would the long-term result be? Propaganda has shaped the response and propaganda of friend and foe alike, influencing the advertising and media industries, and leaving a legacy of sources for historians to argue about and interpret. Here you are asked to look at some examples of propaganda, to judge their aims and messages; to evaluate them for their likely impact and effectiveness, and to consider their value as sources.

## POSTER ART AS PROPAGANDA

A foreign capitalist mocks the 1928 Five Year Plan, but by 1933 is proved wrong

A poster celebrating Stalin's new constitution, 1937

'Only constant repetition will finally succeed in imprinting an idea into the minds of a crowd.'

**Adolf Hitler, Mein Kampf, 1933**

1 What do you think Hitler meant by this statement?
2 How do posters and cartoons use a similar technique?

For further information on the purges, see Hamish Macdonald's *Russia and the USSR: Empire of Revolution* (Longman, 1994).

### Are some types of evidence better than others?

Look at the two sources:

1 If we know that evidence is biased, does it still serve any purpose for historical enquiry?
2 How would you ensure that your use of biased evidence does not distort your interpretation of the past?
3 What do you think he meant would happen to the memory of Stalin in the long term?
4 Why do you think the people of the former Soviet Republics did this?
5 Is the loss of these artefacts and evidence a disaster for historians of the present and the future?

### What is the nature of this evidence?

'No document, and no statement, official or non-official, is beyond question ... it is often important to remember what questions have not been answered. This should not lead to general disbelief, but perhaps to a more general suspension of implicit belief, and to the general habit which makes a man ask of any assertion made to him: What is the nature of the evidence which supports this?

... to that question a second should normally be added: Through whose hands has this evidence passed? '

**G. Kitson Clark, The Critical Historian, 1987**

## THE KEY ISSUES

- What do we mean by 'art as evidence'?
- What different types of 'art as propaganda' exist?
- How can we develop a critical awareness, and the vocabulary needed to work with art and propaganda?

## THE KEY SKILLS

Investigation
Evaluation and interpretation of sources
Critical awareness

## WHAT YOU HAVE TO DO

As a historian, you will need to work with primary and secondary sources of evidence, and you should begin to use the specialised vocabulary that historians use to describe testimony and artefacts from the past.

primary evidence – evidence from a person or period in the past
secondary evidence – histories or commentaries that look back at the past
source – the document or artefact being used
bias – one-sided representations of the past
causation – the reasons why an event happens
provenance – the origin of a source; its background and authenticity

# *Weighing up the Evidence*

Even before the 1917 Revolution, there were over a thousand cinemas across Russia, and urban populations were developing a taste for this new media. The Bolsheviks developed units to exploit film, and 'Agit-trains', special trains converted into mobile cinemas, carried propaganda to the rural areas served by railway lines. They proved both popular and successful. Artistic licence had to be employed by the film-makers, with all shots produced in daylight, and with only limited recourse to special effects. In filming his classic *October*, Eisenstein used live rounds of ammunition, and more people were injured than in the real storming of the Winter Palace!

John Reed, the American journalist who was an eyewitness to the storming of the Winter Palace, wrote:

> 'It was absolutely dark. Over the barricade of firewood we clambered, and leaping down inside gave a triumphant shout as we stumbled on a heap of rifles thrown down by the yunkers [soldiers] who had stood there. On both sides of the gateway the doors stood wide open, light streamed out, and from the huge palace came not the slightest sound.'
>
> **John Reed, Ten Days that Shook the World, 1919**

When the Eisenstein version of events was created, considerably more heroism and drama was brought to bear, and a much more stirring story was created to inspire cinema-goers.

## ART AS PROPAGANDA

Bolshevik and Communist art reflects the artistic mood of the period. Unlike Hitler, the Soviet leadership were initially happy to use the styles of the time, and the artistic representations of the October Revolution and the work of the workers and Red Army reflect styles seen elsewhere in Europe. There were distinct types of propaganda art:

- *The Avant Garde movement*. Artists such as Kazimir Malevich, Vassili Kandinski and Eliezer Lissitsky experimented with new uses of shape and colour, and Russia became the centre for new approaches to art. Their work in attempting to destroy old conventions mirrored the Bolshevik attempt to destroy the 'old' ways of the past regime. They did not always appeal to the conservative tastes of workers and peasants.
- *The school of 'Heroic or Socialist Realism'*. A revised approach in which artists had to portray the heroic efforts of the people, and glorify their contribution to the Bolshevik Revolution. The Association of Artists of Revolutionary Russia flooded Russia with the images and slogans of Communism.
- *Bourgeois art*. Anything that did not glorify the ideals of Communism was seen as deeply suspect. Stalin carried this to an extreme by destroying the work of many individuals. By the 1930s it was unsafe to exhibit or publish works that had not been officially approved. As artists were state-funded, any deviation from the state line could result in withdrawal of sponsorship, and perhaps arrest and deportation.

# THE VALUE OF PROPAGANDA AS SOURCE EVIDENCE

Under Lenin and Stalin, the manipulation of attitudes and minds became an art form, but what is the value to the historian of these biased sources? Propaganda interprets facts and figures selectively and presents an unbalanced picture of the past. History is very much a fragmentary picture of the past, and often we have to use as building blocks fragments of an imperfect record. Being aware from the outset that evidence is not always objective at least gives us the opportunity to see a clear view of one group's' views. Bias need not affect reliability, and need not destroy value, but we must exercise caution and care in interpretation.

F. M. Cornford wrote that 'propaganda is that branch of the art of lying which consists in nearly deceiving your friends without quite deceiving your enemies'. As propaganda is a bold and clearly biased interpretation, those who already hold an opposite view resist its message, while those who sympathise are likely to approve of the message anyway! So, does propaganda work? The Communists certainly thought so. Posters were printed each year with slogans and morals to reflect the events of the time. These show us some of the preoccupations and priorities of different departments of the Communist state. They are also an insight into the literacy of the Soviet people: What images were felt to appeal to the people? What level of simplicity or complexity was felt to be required? Others felt that propaganda only worked while the machinery of state was strong enough to enforce it and prevent anyone from challenging it.

Leon Trotsky, writing in exile, foresaw that despite having a massive propaganda machine Stalin would not be able to preserve a perfect image of himself:

'Nero too, was a product of his epoch, yet after he perished his statues were smashed and his name was scraped off everything. The vengeance of history is more terrible than the most powerful General Secretary. I venture to think that this is consoling.'

*Leon Trotsky, Stalin: an Appraisal of the Man and his Influence (translated by C. Malamuth), 1947; quoted in Stalin's Russia by Chris Ward, 1993*

Propaganda does not make an impact for ever. After his death, Stalin was criticised by former colleagues and his image· quietly sidelined and then removed. During the attempted overthrow of Communism in Hungary (1956), in Czechoslovakia (1968), after the uprisings in the Eastern European Communist states in the 1990s, and after Russia ceased to be a Communist country in 1991, many of the statues of Lenin and Stalin were pulled down by demonstrators, or ordered to be removed by the new governments. Historians may struggle in the future to find busts of Lenin and Stalin, and will find that much of the civic iconography and imagery has been removed and melted down.

## Witting and unwitting evidence

Someone can be aware of the significance or content of what they are saying/recording (witting) or be unaware (unwitting). For example, someone can report a story told to them without realising that it is biased and incorrect: this is unwitting evidence. On the other hand, someone can knowingly report biased evidence, which would provide a witting example of bias.

## Reliability and value

Judgements have to be made as to whether a source can be considered to be trustworthy and reliable – honest and accurate – and whether it is of value. The two are different issues. Unreliable evidence might still tell you a lot, for example about authors and their bias, and so might tell you about the period and events. Reliable evidence might have little value in terms of what you want to find out. Remember that history is fragmentary!

Choose any two of the following types of propaganda: official reports, official statistics, radio broadcasts, posters, leaflets, speeches, portraiture, statues. What are their strengths and weaknesses as historical sources?

## Objective and subjective accounts

Accounts that are based on clear facts and balanced statements are regarded as objective. Those that contain opinion, prejudice and assumptions and are not based on balanced fact are subjective.

## THE KEY ISSUES

- What are the reasons for poor relations between Communist Russia and the West by 1920?
- What happened in the 1920s and 1930s to improve or worsen international relations?

## THE KEY SKILLS

Explanation of events, cause and consequence
Evaluation and assessment

## WHAT YOU HAVE TO DO

Develop an awareness of, and form an opinion on, the significance of:

- the impact of Russia pulling out of the Great War, refusing to honour war debts, and then having to have to fight former allies in the Civil War
- the impact of the policy of trying to incite world revolution, and the anti-Communist backlash this caused
- the series of agreements and minor crises that took place during the 1920s and 1930s
- the way in which the shadow of Nazi Germany looming over Europe eventually forced the USSR and other European states to become allies

# *Understanding International Relations*

The overthrow of the Tsar sent shock waves through the world. Nichola Romanov was related to virtually every ruling royal house in Europe, and h abdication, detention and disappearance, and reports of his death, mad international headlines, as well as causing debate in the governments of th major powers.

After a coup or revolution, other nations have to decide whether to accep the new rulers as the official rulers of the country: if the people support th new regime, the decision is relatively easy. International recognition follow If the overthrown leadership was a 'friendly power' or a democracy that ha been replaced by a dictatorship, or is replaced by a confused situation or civil war, then recognition is not so easy. After the Revolutions, every stat re-evaluated its stance with regard to Russia. Should they recognise the ne regime? Should they take action to intervene in Russian affairs, and if s what would be practical and stand any chance of success? The Bolsheviks di not have majority support, and were anti-democratic, and the internation: community did not recognise their right to rule.

The Bolshevik Party was the only party in the 1917 Provision: Government to seek withdrawal from the Great War. When the Bolshevik agreed the Treaty of Brest–Litovsk, this caused international outrage an resentment. The Russians were not invited to attend the negotiations for th Treaty of Versailles. The Bolshevik government also rejected any debts owe by the previous regimes and refused to pay the huge war debts owed t Russia's allies.

In the Russian Civil War the international community argued about whic 'sides' and factions to support. America's refusal to supply the democrat centre left resulted in a Bolshevik victory, and they were fully aware that th international community would be happy to see them removed from powe The Bolsheviks resented the fact that other states harboured Russian exile and in some cases supported them in vociferous criticism of the new regime Many Bolshevik intellectuals believed that only by encouraging worl revolution would they be secure from foreign intervention. Agents such : Karl Radek were sent to Berlin, Hungary and Austria to incite revolution. I March 1919 the Bolsheviks established the Third (or Communis International to promote world revolution by supporting Communist grou; abroad. Attempts at revolution in Germany, Austria and Hungary failed.

As the Western capitalist economies were in direct opposition to the idea of Communism, mistrust and disputes were perhaps inevitable.

## DID INTERNATIONAL RELATIONS IMPROVE IN THE 1920S AND 1930S?

It is possible to say that there are some signs of the USSR being accepted int the international community: the Communist state was officially 'recognise( as a 'legitimate' government, and a series of international agreements an treaties were signed. Trade also increased – but were relations real improving?

## Arguments in Favour

As the world's first national Communist government gradually gained experience, sympathetic Western leaders attributed the disruption in Russia to 'teething troubles'. Coexistence was possible provided that all countries were prepared to tolerate each other, and not interfere in each other's domestic affairs.

International aid alleviated the suffering of the Civil War, and the famines of the 1920s and 1930s may have eased as foreign powers increased international aid to the USSR.

The USSR began to gain international recognition. The short-lived British Labour government of 1924 did improve relations with the USSR, but was ironically brought down by a scandal caused by 'the Zinoviev Letter' – alleged to be from a member of the Politburo – which urged British Communists to incite revolution in Britain. The 1929–1931 Labour government also improved relations.

## Arguments Against

Not all states tolerated the USSR. Their policy of world revolution frightened many politicians, who foresaw civil war, dictatorship and disaster if Communism spread. In Italy, fear of Communism helped Benito Mussolini to gain power in 1922, and in Germany the fear of the 'red plague' contributed to the weakness of the Weimar Republic, and the rise of extremists such as Adolf Hitler.

In America, the Republicans – the equivalent of Britain's Conservative Party – resented the cost and disruption that they believed involvement in European affairs caused. The Democratic Party of America are somewhere between our Labour Party and the Liberal Democrats, and they also held an anti-Communist stance. The American President at the time of the Revolution was the Democrat Woodrow Wilson, whose dream of involving the USA in world affairs and thus of keeping peace was shattered when the US Senate threw out his plans after the First World War, and when he lost the 1921 election.

Even under Democratic rule before 1941, the USA often followed an isolationist approach to world affairs, and a deep-seated mistrust of all things Communist permeated US foreign policy after 1917.

Co-operation between Germany and the USSR was fostered after they withdrew from the 1922 Genoa Conference and signed the Treaty of Rapallo. This gave the USSR a friendly power between them and the West, and gave Germany the opportunity to manufacture armaments and test military hardware on Soviet territory in secret defiance of the Treaty of Versailles.

Do the events of the period suggest that relations are improving, or are there are signs of trouble 'just around the corner'?

---

### Did outsiders understand the Soviets?

'I cannot forecast to you the action of Russia. It is a riddle wrapped in a mystery inside an enigma; but perhaps there is a key. That key is Russian national interest.'

**Winston Churchill, speech in London, 1 October 1939**

- What do you think Churchill meant?
- In your opinion, why do Westerners often find it difficult to interpret events from a Russian viewpoint?

---

### Key

*appeasement* – the late 1930s policy, followed by Britain and France, of giving in to Hitler's *Lebensraum* ('living space') expansion policy

*isolationism* – the American policy of remaining isolated from world affairs

*Fascism* – a political creed based on: unquestioning nationalism; a deep hatred of socialism/Communism; a militaristic structure; anti-democratic authoritarian policies; and dominant and charismatic leaders (e.g. Hitler and Mussolini)

**THE KEY ISSUES**

- What were the events that led to war in 1941?
- What was the Nazi–Soviet agreement that shocked the world?
- What was Stalin's attitude to Britain and the enemies of Hitler?
- Why did Hitler turn on Stalin?
- Did Stalin underestimate Hitler?

**THE KEY SKILLS**

Explanation of events, cause and consequence
Assessment: role of individuals

**WHAT YOU HAVE TO DO**

Here you should concentrate on the issues of the 1930s and up to 1941. You have some fundamental questions to resolve, such as whether Stalin realised what a danger the Third Reich in Germany was under Hitler, whether Stalin could have avoided war, and whether the USSR should have turned to the West earlier.

You could look at Relations between the USSR and other Powers in the 1930s; or The Nazi–Soviet Pact – What was it, and what was its Significance? Or you could ask Who was to 'Blame' for War in 1939? or Why did Germany and the USSR go to War in 1941?

See Chapter 5, 'Stalin and international relations', in Michael Lynch, *Stalin and Khrushchev – the USSR , 1924–64* (Hodder and Stoughton, 1990); and also A. J. P. Taylor, *The Origins of the Second World War* (Penguin, 1963) and E. Wiskemann, *Europe of The Dictators* (Fontana, 1973).

# *The Road to War*

Causation is a complex subject, and historians rightly see a large number of causes for the Second World War, both short- and long-term. You need to look at the events with regard to the Soviet Union, although an awareness of the wider issues will help to put things into their international context.

## WHAT WERE THE STEPS TO WAR IN 1941?

- Isolated from the international community, the USSR regarded other states as either hostile or indifferent.
- Stalin – although preoccupied with modernising the Soviet economy, the 'war' against the *kulaks* and the purges – also saw the need to prepare the Soviet economy to move rapidly from a peace to a war footing.
- The purges of senior military, diplomatic and civilian ranks left new post-holders without insight or experience.
- International mistrust and poor judgement threw the USSR and Germany together in the 1920s and 1930s. If approaches to the USSR had been more sensitive and those to the Soviets less paranoid, Germany would not have secretly rebuilt its military capacity with Soviet help.
- Disunity failed to prevent pre-Nazi Germany, or Hitler's Germany, from breaching the terms of the Treaty of Versailles.
- In the 1930s various governments were preoccupied with internal affairs, a world-wide recession and a belief that their people would avoid a major war at almost any cost.
- American fear of Communism was enough to prevent any easing of relations with Stalin, but not strong enough to involve them deeply in European affairs until war had begun.

## WHAT WAS STALIN'S ATTITUDE TO BRITAIN AND THE OPPONENTS OF FASCISM?

Communism saw all capitalist nations either as potential trading partners or as critics and enemies. The Depression of the 1930s appears to have convinced Stalin of the need for independence from international trade. But there were still areas of expertise and raw materials that the Soviets could not supply themselves, and many Soviet products were intended for export, to secure much needed foreign currency. As Hitler's power increased, Stalin moved closer to accepting that there were differences between one capitalist state and another. Stalin looked for ways to hold off Nazism by either reaching an understanding with Hitler, or with the West. Many moderate politicians could not believe that Communists and Fascists would be able to reach an agreement.

On 23 August 1939, the Soviet and German Foreign Ministers, Molotov and von Ribbentrop, signed a non-aggression pact in Moscow. Both countries pledged to remain neutral if the other were to go to war. In secret clauses it was agreed that the USSR could annex Bessarabia, Eastern Poland, Estonia, Finland and Latvia; and that Hitler could annex Lithuania and Western Poland.

## WHAT WAS THE SIGNIFICANCE OF STALIN'S ATTITUDE?

Two opposing nations had agreed to put aside their differences in order to gain vast areas of land, keep each other at arms length and secure the other's neutrality. Western and American leaders saw Stalin's actions as a betrayal. But look at this from the Soviet viewpoint: How could this be worse than the shameful treatment of Czechoslovakia by Britain and France, as part of their policy of appeasement? Also they could use their territory as a buffer against future aggression, and bring the benefits of Communism to those they had liberated from capitalism.

'Rendez vous'
A British political cartoon by David Low, published in the London Evening Standard in September 1939

Public opinion was divided. Many wanted to avoid war: memories of the Great War and newsreel scenes from the Italian conquest of Abyssinia and the Spanish Civil War were too fresh in the public mind and, as the British Prime Minister, Neville Chamberlain commented, European trouble did seem a long way away. However, the usual reaction towards Soviet policy in British, French and American newspapers was criticism. Even relatively left-wing newspapers and cartoonists found it hard to accept.

## WAR IN THE WEST!

Hitler had rebuilt his armed forces and tested his foreign policies in the years since 1933, and by 1939 was convinced that Britain and France would offer only token opposition if he acted against Poland. He miscalculated. German forces invaded Poland on 1 September 1939 and Great Britain declared war on Germany on 3 September, but by the end of September Poland was defeated and divided between Germany and the USSR. By the summer of 1940, the Nazis had conquered all of their opponents but Great Britain. Both the USSR and the USA remained neutral.

It seems almost certain that had Hitler concentrated on defeating Great Britain he would have been assured of success. Yet he repudiated the agreements reached with the USSR, ignored the advice of his advisors and, on 22 June 1941, invaded the USSR. Historians give a variety of reasons to explain this action, amongst which are: that neither leader trusted the other; that Hitler feared that the Red Army would declare war and attack at a time of their choosing; that Hitler believed that America would not enter the war, because they were preoccupied with Japan; and that this action was in accord with Hitler's *Lebensraum* ('living space') expansionist policy. Also, the greater part of Europe was under German control, Britain seemed to be about to fall – and Hitler had supreme confidence that his was the superior force and 'race'.

---

### Was conflict inevitable?

'Whereas a year or two ago it was possible and necessary to speak of ... peaceful co-existence between the USSR and the capitalist countries, today ... the period of peaceful co-existence is receding into the past, giving place to a period of imperialist assaults and preparation for intervention against the USSR.'
**Josef Stalin, 1927**

'Hitler invaded Russia for the simple and sufficient reason that he had always meant to establish the foundations of his thousand-year Reich by the annexation of the territory lying between the Vistula and the Urals.'
**Alan Bullock, Hitler – a Study in Tyranny, 1969**

### For discussion and debate

Look at the quotations above. Is it possible that preparation for war by non-aggressive nations makes war more likely, or is it an essential element of defence?

### Did Stalin Underestimate Hitler?

It would be easy to feel that Stalin had been duped by Hitler. Some historians cite comments such as this:

'The tasks of the party are ... to be cautious and not allow our country to be drawn into conflicts by warmongers who are accustomed to have others pull the chestnuts out of the fire for them.'
**Josef Stalin, speech to the Party Congress, 6 January 1941**

## THE KEY ISSUES

- What were the key events of the war?
- What impact did the war have on the USSR?

## THE KEY SKILLS

Explanation of events
Investigation: cause and consequence
Evaluation: source work

## WHAT YOU HAVE TO DO

It is important to be aware of how events shape attitudes, policies and relationships during the war. Your task is to have an overview of the war, and to be clear on the likely impact on Soviet thinking and attitudes.

*Source 1*

*The struggle against Hitler*

*This Soviet cartoon of 1942, by Boris Efimov, is highly critical of the aid being given to the USSR by the Western Allies. Winston Churchill has his feet on a 'Solemn promise to open a second front in Europe during 1942'. In reality, Britain had made no such commitment*

You could examine
The Main Reasons for Soviet Victory;
The Cost of the War; and How the War Affected Soviet Attitudes, the Economy, and Society

# Barbarossa and the Eastern Front

On 22 June 1941, Hitler's forces attacked the Soviet forces and drew the USSR into the Second World War. Despite Stalin's hopes that the Nazi–Soviet Pact would prevent a war, the struggle between Communism and Fascism had begun in earnest. Much of the USSR's key industries and raw materials were vulnerable in the west of the USSR, and – in the early stages of the war – as the Nazi war machine rolled back the Red Army over mile after mile of Soviet territory, things looked bleak for Russia.

Historians agree that the German forces were greatly superior. In *An Economic History of the USSR*, Alec Nove states that 'Germany's economic power was greater than Russia's and she had at her disposal the industries of occupied Europe. Her armies were well equipped, and the equipment had been tested in battle. Despite the very greatest efforts and sacrifices in the preceding decade, the Soviet Union found itself economically as well as militarily at a disadvantage'.

## BLITZKRIEG!

By the end of 1941, German forces had captured 63% of Soviet coal production capacity, 68% of pig iron, 41% of the railway track, 84% of sugar, 38% of grain and 60% of the nation's pigs. Such was the speed of the German advance that there was little time to evacuate much of the occupied area, and yet Soviet records show that over 1500 industrial enterprises had been moved east, of which 1360 were considered to be large-scale. Huge sacrifices were made to send eastwards anything that would help the war effort and deprive the Germans of key prizes, amongst which – from just one steel works, at Zaporozhstal – were 16 000 wagons of equipment, including vital equipment for shaping steel sheet.

*Source 2*

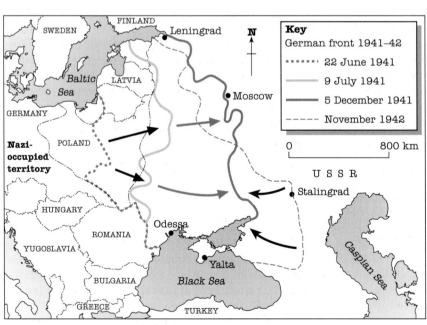

*The campaigns on the Eastern front, 1941–1945*

# EVENTS: 1941–1943

The USSR on the defensive

| | | |
|---|---|---|
| 1941 | 30 June | GKO (Committee For State Defence, supreme government body) established, and runs to 1945 |
| 1941 | 3 July | Stalin makes his first radio broadcast |
| 1941 | September | Leningrad blockaded, Kiev captured by the Germans |
| 1941 | October | Moscow under threat, partial evacuation |
| 1941 | December | Germans pushed back slightly from Moscow |
| 1941 | | Approximately 3 million citizens deported East – most died |
| 1942 | September | The German 6th Army (*Wehrmacht*) reaches and begins the Siege of Stalingrad |
| 1942 | October | The Red Army restores the full status of officer ranks |
| 1942 | November | The Red Army pushes forward and encircles the Germans laying siege to Stalingrad |
| 1943 | January | The Siege of Stalingrad by the Nazis ends in German defeat, with great losses on both sides |

## FIGHTING IN WESTERN EUROPE AND BEYOND

With Britain's survival, the Allies had an armed camp in which to build up their strength. Despite the Battle of the Atlantic, the Battle of Britain and the Blitz, Stalin often suggested that the Allies were not doing enough to help him against the Germans. This is, perhaps, understandable – some American newspapers and cartoonists had shown some delight when the Nazis first attacked the Soviets in 1941, expressing the view that the world would be 'a whole lot better off if the two destroyed each other'. The struggle of the British people and their Allies could be relayed to Stalin, but he would have been much more aware of the suffering of Soviet citizens who were fighting the Nazi war machine. Despite Stalin's criticisms, American lend-lease aid was generous, and the Allies did all they could to meet reasonable Soviet demands in difficult circumstances.

## 'EVERYTHING FOR THE FRONT'

To understand the impact of the war, it is important to examine the level of Soviet sacrifice and effort made during it. The following statistics are intended as a starting point. The Five Year Plans were attempts to modernise the USSR. The war interrupted the third Five Year Plan, and from that moment all production had to be turned over to the war effort. These figures show the levels of production and the way in which the war distorted the economy.

*Source 3*
The war effort. In this table the figures for 1940 are set at 100, so levels above or below this represent growth or decline:

| | 1940 | 1941 | 1942 | 1943 | 1944 |
|---|---|---|---|---|---|
| National income | 100 | 92 | 66 | 74 | 88 |
| Gross industrial output | 100 | 98 | 77 | 90 | 104 |
| Arms industries | 100 | 140 | 186 | 224 | 251 |
| Fuel industries | 100 | 94 | 53 | 59 | 75 |
| Gross agricultural output | 100 | 62 | 38 | 37 | 54 |

*From Istoriya Velikoi otechestvennoi voiny, 1941–45, Vol. VI, quoted in Nove*

*Source 4*
Output (in million tons):

| | 1940 | 1942 | | 1940 | 1942 |
|---|---|---|---|---|---|
| Pig iron | 14.9 | 4.8 | Coal | 165.9 | 75.5 |
| Steel | 18.3 | 8.1 | Oil | 31.1 | 22.0 |
| Rolling mill products | 13.1 | 5.4 | Electricity ($10^9$ kWh) | 48.3 | 29.1 |

*From E. Lokshin, Promyshlennost' SSR 1940–63 (Moscow, 1964)*

1 In what ways might the attitudes shown by the first two quotations have led to the attitude shown in the third quote?
2 How might Stalin have reacted to the final quotation?
3 Do you think that the published views of politicians are always their private views?

## THE KEY ISSUES

- How can we use statistics to summarise and explain historical events?
- What were the impact and legacy of the 'Great Fatherland War', 1941–1945?

## THE KEY SKILLS

Explanation and investigation: events, cause and consequence
Assessment of statistics
Evaluation of sources

## WHAT YOU HAVE TO DO

Try to get to grips with what happened in the war in outline, and try to see how the war would have impacted on the Soviet leadership and shaped their aims for peace and beyond.

### What was the short-term impact of the war?

'… by his onslaught on the Soviet Union, Hitler worked three miracles at once … : he turned irreconcilable enemies, the Soviet Union and the Anglo-Saxons, into allies; he transformed recalcitrant and sullen subjects into Soviet patriots; and he finally persuaded people throughout the world to look upon the Soviet Union as the last bulwark of freedom.'

*Heinrich, Graf von Einsiedel, in*
***The Onslaught: the German Drive to Stalingrad, 1984***

# *General Winter*

Historians have argued about the key turning points of the Second World War. Hitler undoubtedly made his greatest mistake in engaging the Soviets before completing his campaign in the West, underestimating the will of the Soviet people, the strength of the Red Army, and the willingness of Stalin and the Communist leadership to make huge sacrifices. He also rashly declared war on America, a power he had no possibility of defeating.

The battle for Stalingrad is often quoted as a key point: it and certainly wore down German resolve and cost them greatly in terms of manpower and resources. Why and how, then, did the USSR turn the tide? There are two lines of argument: that the Nazis made errors, and that Soviet decision making and good luck intervened.

## NAZI ERRORS

- *Ambition instead of strategy*. Hitler relied on a rapid campaign and attacked in June. Despite huge advances, his forces were eventually halted.
- *Poor planning*. German equipment was incapable of coping with the Russian winter. Also, they had overstretched communications and supply lines.
- *German tactics and brutality*. Atrocities by SS units united the peasants against the invading forces.
- *Hitler's role*. He interfered in military decision-making, and made poor strategic choices.

## SOVIET ACTION

- *Determination and sacrifices*. Soviet policy was to destroy anything of use to the enemy. Guerrilla units then disrupted the invaders as they advanced. Millions died in slowing the German advance.
- *Patriotism*. Despite the purges and low morale, the Red Army troops were fighting for their way of life and the survival of their nation and families.
- *Able Soviet generals*. The generals were allowed to pursue their plans without undue interference from Stalin.
- *Stalin*. With the economy on a war footing, the centrally planned economy kept the war effort going.
- *Specific battles*. Some battles were major boosts to Soviet morale: Moscow held out in the summer of 1942; Leningrad was besieged from 1942 to 1944; and Stalingrad was besieged by 21 German Divisions. Eventually 90 000 surviving German troops surrendered in February 1943. Millions of ordinary Soviet citizens died in the fighting.

## KEY EVENTS

The Red Army was able to advance by the summer of 1943, with a successful push in the Ukraine, and German retreats during 1944. Romania and Finland, which had sided with Hitler, then surrendered, followed by Hungary in January 1945. Romania, Bulgaria, the Baltic states and Austria were occupied. In Yugoslavia, the Partisan leader Marshal Tito led an uprising, and defeated the occupying forces. Poland was liberated, and the Red Army pushed into East Germany and besieged Berlin in April 1945. Germany unconditionally surrendered on 7 May.

There are no totally reliable figures for Soviet war dead, as the statistics have to account for civilians killed by the weather, starvation and by the enemy, as well as actual combatants. Current estimates put the figure at

20–25 million. To this should be added the millions whose lives and livelihoods, families and whole circumstances had been destroyed or disrupted. We know that the Germans executed or caused the deaths of at least 1 million Russian Jews and 2.9 million Polish Jews, with a further 700 000 from Czechoslovakia and Romania also killed.

## CO-OPERATION AND POSTWAR PLANNING

The Allied powers engaged in a series of major planning meetings during the war, sometimes led by the national leaders, but often by military leaders and civilian planners. The most famous of these are the Yalta and Potsdam Conferences. At Yalta, in February 1945, Roosevelt, Stalin and Churchill met to discuss their final objectives for the war and to coordinate their efforts. By August 1945, at Potsdam, Britain had a new Labour Prime Minister, Clement Attlee (Churchill having lost the General Election) and America had a new President, Harry Truman, who took over after the death of Roosevelt. Here the leaders discussed the peace settlement with regard to Germany, and the related issues.

## THE ALLIED CONTRIBUTION

America operated a policy of lend-lease aid to Britain before 1941, in which goods and military hardware were provided on a pay-for-it-later basis. When the USSR joined the war, the USA extended this policy to them. Despite their own difficulties in supply and gaining raw materials, the Allied leaders recognised the sacrifice that the Russian people were making to carry on the war against the Nazis. Convoys were sent on perilous journeys to the Arctic, to supply materials to the Red Army and people. It was in the interests of the West to show that they were being supportive, and of Stalin not to acknowledge the level of support publicly. These figures show some of the items imported, but cannot measure the human cost of getting them to the USSR.

*Source 5*

Imports from Allied countries, 1941–1945:

| Guns | 9 600 |
| Planes | 18 700 |
| Tanks | 10 800 |

*Source 6*

Lend-lease (from USA), 1941–1945:

| Machine tools | 44 600 |
| Railway locomotives | 1 860 |
| Non-ferrous metals | 517 500 tons |
| Cable and wire | 172 100 tons |

## WHAT WAS IMPACT AND LEGACY OF THE 'GREAT FATHERLAND WAR', 1941–1945?

*Source 7*

The cost of the war:

| | Number of war dead (millions) | Cost (£ million) |
|---|---|---|
| USSR | 20 | 48 000 |
| USA | 0.4 | 84 500 |
| Great Britain | 0.4 | 28 000 |
| Germany | 4.2 | 68 000 |

*From Jack Watson, Success in Twentieth Century World Affairs, 1984*

### Is History the truth?

'The victor will not be asked if he told the truth or not. In starting and waging a war it is not right that matters, but victory.'
*Adolf Hitler, quoted in William L. Shirer, The Rise and Fall of the Third Reich, 1960*

In this quotation, Hitler is giving his views on the value of propaganda and mis-information, which can, he believed, be valuable weapons. During the war Stalin made many complaints that the USSR was being forced to struggle on with relatively little aid from the West.

1 Why might Stalin not admit how much Western aid he was really receiving?
2 Why might wartime figures and statistics from either side be unreliable?

*Source 8*

A Russian cartoon from the 30 August 1945 issue of the magazine Krokodil

*The world is personified and is happily giving itself a close shave. On the towel, the swastikas represent the fact that the German threat has already been removed, and Japan is just about to be shaved away*

Use the same headings as the key issues above, and add a section in which you look at what happened in the 'liberated' nations of Eastern Europe from 1945 to 1953. (You might find it helpful to research aspects of postwar Eastern Europe in more detail.)

**The leader**

'I trust no one, not even myself.'

*Josef Stalin, 1951*

In what ways does Stalin's treatment of the Eastern European states, Communist parties and returning prisoners or war demonstrate that Stalin did not trust anyone?

# Europe Divided

## WHY WAS EUROPE DIVIDED BETWEEN THE USSR AND THE WEST AFTER THE WAR?

Throughout the war, diplomats, military advisors and the leaders of the main combatants met on a regular basis to discuss tactics and policy. At the conferences at Yalta in February 1945 and Potsdam in August 1945, plans were discussed for the closing stages of the war and the immediate period thereafter.

At Yalta, the Allied leaders agreed map locations where their forces would 'stop' while liberating Europe, preventing accidental clashes between friendly forces. This divided Europe into sectors occupied by the Americans, French and British in the west, and areas occupied by the Red Army in the east. The arrangement was intended to be temporary, but neither side showed any keenness to withdraw their forces.

There are always costs in reaching diplomatic compromises, and at Yalta this was to prove to be a human cost. Britain agreed at Yalta to repatriate all Soviet prisoners or refugees on Allied sector soil. Thousands of men, women and children were shot immediately by the Red Army or died later in Soviet labour camps.

*Source 1*

'... the Cossack Officers scrambled onto the British trucks with their minds gyrating like anguished savages. It was like wartime all over again: people were saying goodbye to each other; wild eyed officers' wives were weeping, amazed at the sudden and furious disturbance; their screaming children hung onto their fathers' jackets.

When the transport returned empty without the Cossacks, the very air struck terror ... a combination of tempers and prayers raged through the night. Worse still, in the gaping darkness, one of the officers who had somehow managed to escape crawled back into the camp. Lifeless and badly bleeding about the chest, pulsating saliva running from the corners of his mouth, he delivered his gigantic curses to the faces around him.

The British have lied and betrayed us  he sobbed. His thin body vibrated from weakness, but he carried on talking:  The Soviets snarled at our men like wolves and then shot them in the woods. We were handed over to ...  He suddenly lurched forward and lapsed into silence.'

*Zoe Polanska-Palmer, Yalta Victim, 1988*

## WHAT CHANGES DID STALIN MAKE IN SOVIET-OCCUPIED EUROPE?

Soviet forces dismantled some of the industries in occupied territories and sent materials home as reparation for the disruption to the Soviet economy. Communist parties in these territories were resurrected, with pro-Stalinist leaders in charge, and the occupied states elected Communist governments. Russia had been invaded repeatedly throughout its history, and Stalin was convinced that the only way to prevent this from happening in the future was for the USSR effectively to create a series of buffer or satellite states.

After the war, the world was keen to ensure that the mistakes of the earlier Treaty of Versailles were not repeated, and keeping the USSR as an active member of the international community was seen as a major stepping stone in securing future peace. Consequently, the USSR became a full member of the United Nations, took a permanent seat on the Security Council (the body that manages international crises) and was given a veto over emergency action.

# THE THIN PRETENCE OF FRIENDSHIP SLIPS

The new Communist empire arising from liberated territories worried Western Europe and America. Revolution had failed to convince Europe to turn to Communism, but now the Red Army and Soviet 'advisors' were potentially able to complete the task. America and the USSR dominated the world in 1945, but soon fell out.

*Source 2*

'Hitler had frightened them into each other's arms and it could hardly be expected that they would remain in close embrace, once he had disappeared. They proceeded to harbour extravagant apprehensions against each other. Both operated from fear. The Americans from fear of communism, the Russians from fear of nuclear weapons ... essentially the attitude of the two world powers towards Europe was unchanged: they merely wanted Europe to leave them alone.'

**A. J. P. Taylor, From Sarajevo to Potsdam, 1966**

*Source 3*

A Russian cartoon from the late 1940s

The signs in front of the delegates read (left to right) Luxembourg, Holland, Belgium, France and Great Britain

*Source 4*

Who's next to be liberated from freedom?

A British cartoon from March 1949, by David Low – after imposing a Communist regime on Czechoslovakia, Stalin and Molotov plan the next move

Sources 3 and 4 show neatly how both the USSR and the West saw things in almost mirror-image terms: both thought that the other was a dangerous and interfering power, determined to secure its own aims at the expense of everyone else.

# EXPORTING COMMUNISM

One of the major features of the 1930s had been the Fascist use of scare stories about the 'red peril' – the idea that Stalin wanted to sweep across Europe and create a Red Empire. The fact that Bolshevik leaders such as Trotsky favoured international revolution had helped to create a fear of Communism. The Comintern, seen as a cover for spying and agitation, had been disbanded in 1943 to show good will towards the Western Allies during the war.

However, in 1947 Stalin again seemed to be keen to export Communism, and the Cominform (Communist Information Bureau) was created. It was designed to coordinate the external propaganda and policies of the Communist parties of the Eastern European Communist states. In the West it was seen as an excuse to cause trouble abroad, and as a way of encouraging malcontents and agitators. In reply, Stalin complained that there was constant foreign interference in Soviet affairs, and that the Cominform had peaceful and positive intentions.

**The eye-witness** ?

Read the extract from Zoe Polanska-Palmer's book *Yalta Victim* (Source 1). This account is taken from a powerful series of memories and observations about the repatriation of prisoners of war, refugees and others to the Soviet Union.

1 Does the fact that the person who wrote it was there, and clearly feels that the British and Soviet actions were unethical, alter the value of this and other similar evidence?

2 Is subjective evidence less useful than objective evidence? Explain your view.

Find out more about this and similar incidents with Polish and other nationalities if you can.

See the section on the Cold War in Michael Lynch, *Stalin and Khrushchev – the USSR 1924–64* (Hodder and Stoughton, 1990) and Isaac Deutscher, *Stalin* (Pelican, 1966). See also Zoe Polanska-Palmer, *Yalta Victim* (Grafton, 1988). This is a moving first-hand account based on one woman's experience of surviving deportation from captured Soviet territory to Auschwitz, liberation and near deportation back to the USSR.

## THE KEY ISSUES

- What was the Cold War and why did it begin?
- What are the main Cold War events between 1945 and 1953?
- What legacy did Stalin leave for Russia and the world?

## THE KEY SKILLS

Assessment: causes and consequences
Research

## WHAT YOU HAVE TO DO

Look at the reasons that explain why the East and West fell out, and the impact that this had on Europe and the wider world in the 1940s and early 1950s.

### Hot spots of the Cold War

- The satellite states – 'democracies' set up in Soviet-occupied territories
- Civil war in Greece in 1946
- The Truman Doctrine, which committed the USA to intervening, with aid or deed, wherever Communist forces were attempting to take over the state
- The Marshall Plan, to give economic aid to Western Europe – in response the USSR set up Comecon
- The Berlin Blockade of 1948, which led to the Berlin airlift
- NATO – established by the Western states in 1949 to pledge mutual military assistance
- Purges in the satellite states
- Atomic espionage – the first Soviet A-bomb was tested in 1949; the USA claimed that the USSR had stolen the technology
- The Korean War, 1950–1953, in which the Communist North invaded the South – the country had been partitioned in 1945

# Behind and Beyond the Iron Curtain

## WHAT IS THE IRON CURTAIN?

To prevent interference in Soviet affairs and in the new Communist states, Stalin once again restricted the access of foreigners to the USSR and the satellite states, almost drawing a curtain of secrecy between capitalist Europe and Communist Europe. The image of an 'iron curtain' shielding Russia from the critical gaze of outsiders had been used before, but it was Churchill who was to popularise it fully.

In February 1945, Hitler's Propaganda Minister, Josef Goebbels, had correctly predicted the postwar division of Europe when he said 'Should the German people lay down its arms the agreement between Roosevelt, Churchill and Stalin would allow the Soviets to occupy all Eastern Europe and South-eastern Europe together with the major part of the Reich. An iron curtain would at once descend on this territory, which including the Soviet Union would be of enormous dimensions.'

## THE COLD WAR

The division of Europe between a Soviet Bloc and a Western Alliance was to shape Europe and dominate world politics for the next 40 years, would influence diplomacy across the globe, and would cause conflict and rivalry in a way never seen before. To understand the 'Cold War' you have to remind yourselves of three key features of thinking:

- The Soviet approach to outsiders was to look at past experience – foreign powers were invariably hostile and aggressive, despite their attempts to appear otherwise.
- The USSR had suffered enormously in order to reconstruct itself and transform the lives of its people. Such gains would not lightly be given up.
- Communism was, the leadership believed, the solution to the problem of chaotic and confused world affairs and economies – not part of the problem.

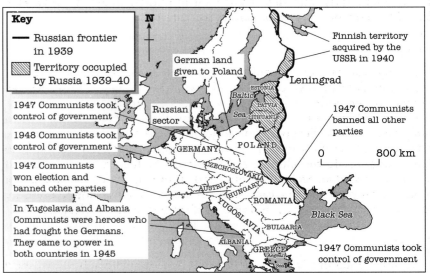

Soviet buffer states created in Europe from 1945
[Russia pledges to] 'grant the liberated peoples of Europe the full right and freedom to decide for themselves the question of their form of government'.
Josef Stalin, speaking in 1943

# THE END OF AN ERA?

On 1 March 1953, the 73-year-old Stalin suffered a brain haemorrhage, followed by a stroke and paralysis. He lost his speech and consciousness. On 5 March, Stalin died, and his death was announced in the next day's news bulletins. The last few days of his life had given his closest advisors the time to decide how to rule the USSR. Malenkov became Prime Minister and, with a small group of senior party members, ruled by committee. Isaac Deutscher wrote:

> 'According to all accounts, the nation reacted to the event with the contradictory moods which Stalin's complex and ambiguous personality inspired: some wept in anguish, others sighed with relief; most were stunned and afraid to think of the future. His successors walked warily. They had been Stalin's mere shadows. They were not inclined to pay the dead man the fulsome tribute they had paid the living; and they were terrified of not paying it.'
>
> **Isaac Deutscher, Stalin, 1966**

Within a few short years, some of his closest supporters during his life would be denouncing him, or disgraced themselves. Trotsky had been right when he said that idols do not last for ever.

# WHAT WAS STALIN'S LEGACY?

## The Economy

Stalin had not solved the USSR's food shortages problems, but the economy was considerably stronger, and progress had been made in making the USSR independent of outside technology. However, this had been achieved by building a culture of dependency.

## The People

In effect, Stalin had created a police state in which even blatant abuse of Party privilege and denouncing stupidity was dangerous. Many Soviet citizens had learnt to their cost that it was unwise to even voice criticism of the state and Party, and that it was fatal to criticise Stalin. Citizens were denied freedom of expression, movement and work.

## The Party

The Party leadership who had worshipped Stalin while he was alive now began the difficult task of ruling without him. Nikita Khrushchev, an enthusiastic supporter of the Moscow purges of the 1930s, became Party Leader and Prime Minister and – without relaxing Party discipline – eased aside the group of colleagues who had jointly taken over after Stalin's death. Beria, Stalin's faithful Chief of Police, was arrested and shot. At the 1956 Party Congress, Khrushchev secretly criticised Stalin's rule, revealed that Lenin had wished for Stalin's removal, and ordered the release of millions of political prisoners from the camps. When this news was leaked to others, it caused worldwide headlines, and ripples of concern in the Soviet leadership.

## Europe

The Cold War was firmly under way at the time of Stalin's death. It continued as if he were still alive, and – to adapt the closing comment of Isaac Deutscher's book *Stalin* – his successors were perplexed by the legacy of his rule yet still unable to master and transcend it, and for the time being sought merely to follow the route that Stalin had helped to create.

## A climate of mistrust ...

'[Roosevelt] ... soon became convinced that he could get on better with Stalin than he did with Churchill and was therefore ready to accept Russia as a partner in running the world.'

**A. J. P. Taylor, From Sarajevo to Potsdam, 1966**

'There's nothing they [the English] like better than to trick their allies ... Churchill is the kind of man who will pick your pocket of a kopek ... if you don't watch him ... And Roosevelt? Roosevelt is not like that. He dips his hand in only for bigger coins.'

**Josef Stalin, 1945 (but not made public at the time)**

'The reason for having diplomatic relations is not to confer a compliment, but to secure a convenience.'

**Winston Churchill, House of Commons, 17 November 1949**

1  In what ways do the above quotations help to explain the climate of mistrust between the Allied powers during the war and afterwards?

2  Stalin said 'There must be a minimum moral standard between all nations ... nations must fulfil their treaty obligations, otherwise international society will be unable to survive'. Do you think Stalin's policy towards, and actions in, Eastern Europe between 1945 and 1953 were moral and acceptable? Explain your answer.

Use the key issues and supplement these by looking at the hot spots of the cold war section. Your additional research should look at any of the hot spots that you feel are especially significant, or might help explain any other topics that you will study.

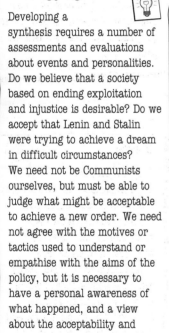

### Making judgements

Developing a synthesis requires a number of assessments and evaluations about events and personalities. Do we believe that a society based on ending exploitation and injustice is desirable? Do we accept that Lenin and Stalin were trying to achieve a dream in difficult circumstances? We need not be Communists ourselves, but must be able to judge what might be acceptable to achieve a new order. We need not agree with the motives or tactics used to understand or empathise with the aims of the policy, but it is necessary to have a personal awareness of what happened, and a view about the acceptability and ethical issues involved.

These pages are a personal synthesis of some of the key aspects of the issues we have looked at in the book so far. You might disagree with the emphasis on certain issues or feel that some key elements have been neglected, but history is about making interpretations. There will inevitably be a subjective as well as an objective element in any reconstruction and interpretation of the past.

# Synthesis

## 1. What Brought About the End of the Monarchy?

Although in crisis in 1917, the Romanov Empire – which had survived previous emergencies – was removed by the two Revolutions, which also restructured society.

The urban workers and intellectuals unseated the Tsar in February 1917. The liberal and democratic regime of the Provisional Government was in power, but seemed unsure of its authority to rule. The Russian people had great expectations for a dramatic improvement in their lives, but largely received the post-revolutionary shock of unaccomplished aspirations. The Provisional Government could not deliver what everyone wanted, and stumbled from crisis to crisis.

The Provisional Government failed to deal firmly with dissent or to realise the futility of continuing the Great War, and by October 1917 Russia remained ripe for further unrest. The Bolsheviks gambled on the support of local workers, soldiers and sailors, and that the democratic opposition would largely be reluctant to respond with force. Also, the inertia of the mass of the population made for only a very small enemy in the short term.

The Bolsheviks were prepared to take risks and seize opportunities with a single-minded approach, despite internal policy differences. They overthrew a weak government and assumed that the urban workers would accept a new approach, and that the rural population was too isolated to oppose them. They were right. Power was gained without a legal mandate to rule or any semblance of majority support.

## 2. Why did the Bolsheviks Gain and Retain Power?

The Bolsheviks promised to give the people what they wanted, and set about establishing strict discipline and control. Democratic reform was rapidly set aside when the results suggested that a moderate government would replace the Bolsheviks. Lenin dissolved the assembly, and a Bolshevik dictatorship began. Withdrawal from the war was rapidly negotiated, and the Bolsheviks consolidated their control over the cities and extended their power. This resulted in a repressive regime being established, its extremist measures hastened by the Civil War, economic hardship, international isolation and the famines of the 1920s.

Lenin was pragmatic enough to secure control over the state before attempting to develop a centrally planned and led economy based on Communist principles. Central control was limited, despite the nationalisation of industry, and a firmer direction was given to the economy. Most notable were the early attempts to reshape society and create a Communist Utopia. Titles – and ranks in the military – were abolished, and family law was relaxed and liberalised. Although high philosophy often foundered on the conservative nature of the Russian people and the problems that the Bolshevik 'empire' had acquired from its predecessors, progress was made and society began to show the effects of Communist-style policies, and a Communist attitude and belief structure.

## 3. Why and how did Stalin Succeed Lenin?

From Lenin's death in 1924 to Trotsky's exile in 1929, Stalin had been quietly working to secure the personal loyalty of the Politburo members and key members of the government. His grasp of pragmatic politics, and the use of purges, the secret police and ruthless tactics, made him universally feared – and if not respected, at least regarded with caution and reservation. The USSR adopted the same model that appeared in Italy under Mussolini and in Germany under Hitler – extremist government by a single party and by a totally ruthless dictator. Policy became the whim of a single person, advised by a small group of nervous close confidants, and the will of the people was subsumed by the glorification and interests of one individual.

More scholarly research could continue into the role of other leading figures. The post-Leninist phase has blurred the impact of other individuals. Stalin worked hard to enhance his own position, and to ensure that others were represented less favourably. Addressing the role of other figures will be part of the work of future historians.

## 4. What was it Like to Live in Stalinist Russia?

The years from 1929 to 1953 represent all that is worst and best about Communism in the USSR in the 20th century. It was a time of sacrifice and hardship: of a battle against supposed and real enemies of the state; of an unnecessary conflict with capitalist nations through the Cold War and the arms race.

Domestic policy was secondary to control and discipline, and although life must have had few lighter moments for many, the Russian people were nothing if not resilient. Can we state with any certainty that life under Stalin was worse than in the shambolic Tsarist autocracy?

Despite progression in its economy and agricultural production, gains were patchy, often short-lived and achieved at great human cost. In the 20 years during which he was in power, we would expect Stalin's society to change and progress, but Stalin kept Russia frozen in a time warp. Others did the decision-making and the workers had merely to obey. The workers lost their chains under Marxism, and their right to self-expression and self-determination under Stalinism.

There are undoubtedly reasons for Stalin's paranoia, perhaps the greatest being the threat of fascism and the Second World War, which turned Europe upside down. In Russia, the estimates for civilian and military war dead run to 20–25 million citizens, and countless others who were displaced, desolate and dispossessed. Russia suffered devastation, and yet was able to build a new empire that lasted for a further 50 years.

The USSR was both weakened and strengthened by Stalin, and given a lasting legacy in the shape of what Stalin had put in place – much of which would outlive him.

## 5. What was the Stalinist Legacy for the USSR?

Stalin was succeeded by men cast in his own image, products of the Communist Party machine, and schooled to think, act and believe along certain set lines. Despite the rigour with which Stalin chose his underlings, Khrushchev – leader from 1955 to 1964 – liberalised internal affairs and offered peaceful coexistence to the West. Leonid Brezhnev – leader from 1964 to 1982 – was more hard-line, reintroduced repressive measures at home, and pursued the Cold War with some vigour but considerable caution.

## 6. Reform ... and the End?

By the 1980s under Mikhail Gorbachev the Soviet Union was still unable to meet its people's needs and desires, and the Communist structure collapsed, as a reforming leadership was challenged by hard-line Communists. The USSR disintegrated.

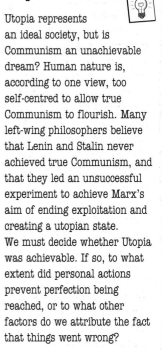

### Extrapolation and synthesis

Historians are shaped by the preoccupations of the period in which they write. To reach a synthesis they have to examine sources and select the relevant information to support their enquiry. This process of drawing relevant information together is called 'extrapolation'. Individuals can make their interpretation of the past through a 'synthesis' – a personal view of the past and the significance of events and personalities.

Writing about Russia in the 20th century is not cut and dried. There is still scope for individual interpretation, to establish your own viewpoint and support it – to establish your dialogue with the past!

### Utopia

Utopia represents an ideal society, but is Communism an unachievable dream? Human nature is, according to one view, too self-centred to allow true Communism to flourish. Many left-wing philosophers believe that Lenin and Stalin never achieved true Communism, and that they led an unsuccessful experiment to achieve Marx's aim of ending exploitation and creating a utopian state.

We must decide whether Utopia was achievable. If so, to what extent did personal actions prevent perfection being reached, or to what other factors do we attribute the fact that things went wrong?

# *Argument*

## 1. Why were there Two Russian Revolutions in 1917?

To respond successfully, you have to be able to write about the causes of the February Revolution, the arrival and work of the Provisional Government, and the reasons why this fell in October to the Bolsheviks.

**There are many, complex long- and short-term causes, about which historians disagree. My triggers are causes that remain after the first (February) Revolution to cause the second (October) Revolution:**

|  | 1. Weak government | 2. Unpopular | 3. Massive urban discontent | 4. The war as a catalyst |
|---|---|---|---|---|
| February | Tsar's past record:<br>● Seen as unreliable, a poor performer, and a weak and incompetent leader | ● Not seen as a man who would act<br>● Widespread hardship | ● Poverty<br>● Price inflation<br>● Food shortages<br>● Awful home and work conditions<br><br>= political agitation | ● Draining effect<br>● Low morale<br>● Unrest in military<br>● Impact on Russian people and popularity of the Tsar |
| October | Provisional Government<br>● Lacklustre performance<br>● Many members with conflicting interests | ● Liberal policies encourage critics<br>● Weaknesses exposed by the Kornilov Plot and the July Days | ● Expectations raised by February Revolution ... but not fulfilled | ● Only the Bolsheviks promise to end the war! |

**A too liberal government failing to respond to basic human needs**

*Essay plan 1*

This plan is an attempt to acknowledge that, with hindsight, many things can be seen to be the causes of great events. Some may seem insignificant at the time of the events themselves, and historians disagree about which were the most significant. The main thrust of the argument is that the same general problems that overthrew the Tsar encouraged the Bolsheviks to topple the Provisional Government.

Rather than narrate lots of causes and consequences in a list of what happened when and why, the idea is to deal with the themes shown – leadership, policies, the war, urban discontent – and a series of domestic issues, and show that they contributed to both revolutions. The argument can be built that until a government dealt with Russia's problems – or suppressed dissent (and gained time to tackle the problems) – further trouble was inevitable.

The Provisional Government was weak in the sense that it was liberal and progressive, and allowed others to continue to agitate and act. Its own good intentions brought it down.

Your conclusion should draw together the arguments that you have made and answer the question.

# 2. To what Extent was Lenin a Red Tsar, who Created a Regime Based on Terror and Repression, with Little Real Improvement for the People?

This question is about the policy and actions of Lenin's government to 1924, and asks you to look at what changed in Russia under Lenin and whether things improved for the people. Was Lenin just doing what previous rulers of Russia had done, or was there a different sense of vision and purpose behind his actions? What harsh measures were used to govern Russia? Were they justified? Did they improve the lives, or life chances, of the people?

*1. You need to define the term 'Red Tsar'*

*2. What were Lenin's aims/ needs?*
- To work within the existing system and reform when circumstances allowed
- To maintain control in Soviet-held territory and expand/promote world revolution
- To defeat or hold off anti-Communist forces, counter-revolutionaries and enemies of the state

*3. Why were repressive measures required to achieve these aims?*

| Minority party – the Bolsheviks did not have majority support | Minority of Russia – support was centred in urban areas | The Civil War – large areas outside of Lenin's control | Revolts – Kronstadt and others | The economy – Communism watered down by War Communism and NEP |
|---|---|---|---|---|

*4. What repressive measures were used?*

| Red Guard | 'Law and order' – secret police legal system labour camps | Propaganda – speeches    posters slogans    censorship agit trains + boats | Famine – Allowed to impact on certain areas |
|---|---|---|---|

*5. Were these measures, based on the scale of problems, justified?*
- What other less repressive things happened?
- Did Russia benefit or suffer?    • What do historians say?

*6. Conclusion*
- Did the means justify the ends?
- Did Lenin use a system that he inherited?
  - **Sum up your argument and answer the question**

*Essay plan 2*

This plan gives you the chance to define the term 'Red Tsar' and to develop an argument that looks at Lenin's aims and intentions – and his practical needs. The thrust of my argument would be that Lenin was a pragmatic and brilliant thinker. He re-established some structures taken from the Tsars, but which the Provisional Government had swept away. Look at his reasons for this (the problems that Bolshevik Russia faced) and the tools used to hold on to power.

Either as you progress, or separately, ensure that you answer the part of the question that asks if there was any improvement in the lives of the people. What benefits might justify the loss of freedom? Is it acceptable to be repressive if this protects the state in a crisis? Can minorities be allowed to suffer for the benefit of the majority? Is dictatorship an acceptable form of government?

Use the facts that you know, and the comments of other historians, to support your answers to these issues, and build an answer to the question. Be careful not to crusade against injustice and repression: you are entitled to make some comments, but do not let value judgements take the place of historical argument. Draw together your arguments in your conclusion – and answer the question!

---

## Opinions of Lenin: an evidence-based question

*Source 1*

'Lenin did not hesitate for a single instant to revive the worst traditions of despotism.'

**The Times, 23 January 1924**

*Source 2*

'Lenin cared not at all for the people or the improvement in their condition, but only for his theories and the power to try them out … in my view the man was a monster.'

**From the autobiography of Elisaveta Fen, Remember Russia 1915–25, quoted in Tom Corfe's Russia's Revolutions (1989)**

*Source 3*

'Lenin stands for all those qualities – purposefulness, realism, common sense, will power, pugnacity – which were most lacking in the pre-Revolutionary intelligentsia.'

**Christopher Hill, Lenin and the Russian Revolution, 1947**

Read Sources 1 and 2:

**1** Are these sources in favour of, or against Lenin? (4 marks)

**2** Does the fact that these sources were written and published in Britain affect their value and reliability? If so, how and why? (4 marks)

Read Source 3:

**3** Does Source 3 support or contradict the previous sources? (4 marks)

With reference to these and any other sources of primary evidence:

**4** Is it possible that all three sources are correct, or is it likely that one or more sources are incorrect? (6 marks)

**5** Is it true that openly biased evidence is of limited value to an historian? (7 marks)

## 3. How and why did Stalin Establish and Maintain a Dictatorship in the USSR from 1929 to 1953?

This task calls for a structured account to show how Stalin secured and maintained his power base in Russia, his motives and techniques, and the ways in which other circumstances helped or hindered his actions.

In some ways, it is like the previous question on Lenin's methods, and will give you the chance to write about whether Stalin is similar to or different from Lenin in his approach. It should also give you the chance to think about another question which is sometimes asked: Does Stalin continue Lenin's work?

*1. Repressive measures existed already*
- Climate of fear  • Labour camps  • One-party state  • Censorship
- Propaganda  • Centralisation  • Secret police

*2. How and why were they strengthened?*

| Rivalry with Trotsky | Mistrust of others | Need for USSR to develop – | DO OUTSIDE EVENTS MAKE STALIN NECESSARY AND GIVE HIM AN EXCUSE TO ACT? | Surrounded by loyal and uncritical supporters | Personal paranoia | Force of character – |
|---|---|---|---|---|---|---|
| • Expulsion  • Exile  • Murder (1940) | • Kirov murder  • Purges: –show trials –camps –supporters put into power | • Economy  • Fears of foreign powers: growing German threat, 1933–1941; war, 1941–1945  = Cold War climate | | • Was the Politburo convinced that USSR was at risk of collapse and/or invasion? | | • No-one stood up to him successfully  • Fear of *Gulags* |

    ○ Use historians' views to support your argument ... AND use examples to back up your argument not drive it!

*3. The result?*  • A CLIMATE OF FEAR – but one in which the senior figures continued to co-operate with Stalin
       • Can we blame one man ... or are others to blame?
       • Was the 'West' at fault?
         ○ **Draw your arguments to a conclusion ... summarising your views and responding to the question**

*Essay plan 3*

The plan here begins with the premise that Stalin acquired the mechanism for dictatorship, but extended it and used it more extensively than Lenin. The argument is that Stalin faced fewer external threats (before the late 1930s) than Lenin, and that he therefore turned inward and saw enemies within the USSR.

The essay looks at how and why this took place. Ensure that you comment on these issues together – it will give you an analytical base rather than a narrative one. Look at the facts as a way of supporting your argument as to why Stalin was so unsettled, and what he did as a result. Avoid temptations to preach on a 'how awful it all was' line of argument. Make a point, support it, and move on!

Your conclusion should draw together the themes that you have developed, and pull them into a summary that answers the question. Trying to recap on the *how* aspect of the question will just give you a repeat of the features of Stalin's rule, and so it is probably better to run through the *why*, drawing out the key reasons for Stalin's actions – and stating your own interpretation.

# 4. Is it True that in the Period 1929–1941 Stalin's Five Year Plans Failed to Transform the Economy of the USSR, and made no Impact on the Soviet Union?

This question requires consideration of the impact and success of the Five Year Plans, and asks you to assess what sort of impact they had on the USSR. Stronger answers will argue a case rather than try to blind the examiner with statistics or narration.

*1. Why was there a need for an economic transformation?*

| Political/philosophical problems – | Practical problems |
|---|---|
| • Undesirability of relying on capitalist trade and occasional famine relief<br>• Need to increase public contentment and confidence<br>• The NEP was not 'true Communism' | • Economic backwardness<br>• Agricultural inefficiency<br>• Lack of self-sufficiency |

*2. What were the aims of the FYPs?*

| Industry – | Agriculture – | TO MAKE THE USSR SELF-SUFFICIENT | Achieved by means of – |
|---|---|---|---|
| • Heavy industry<br>• Raw materials | • Collectivisation | | • Central planning of economy<br>• Justify repression<br>• Focusing on wreckers and *kulaks* – public enemies |

*3. Did the FYPs work?* • Give *your* observations and interpretation
    ○ Remember to comment on the reliability of evidence that we have, and say what historians think of the FYPs

*4. The debate: What was the immediate impact to 1941?*

| Did the FYPs help the USSR prepare for the Second World War?<br>• Would this justify harshness? | What was their impact on the wider economy? | To what extent did they give Stalin an excuse for:<br>• Purges?<br>• Terror attacks? | What was the impact on ordinary citizens? | To what extent did the FYPs hit other policies? |
|---|---|---|---|---|

*5. What was the longer-term impact of the FYPs (after 1941)? [Make a brief mention only!]*
    • The plans have an impact up to 1941 in that they are continued after 1945 so the idea hasn't been discredited ... and the new Communist states also go for centrally planned economies
        ○ **Draw the points and the general tone of your argument together, and answer the question in your final paragraphs**

*Essay plan 4*

You need to decide, in your opinion, whether or not the Five Year Plans were a good thing for the USSR – then you can construct a case that supports your view rather than rambles! Also, remember that it is fine to use the views of historians with a different perspective as well as those who support your view.

    My plan here attempts to establish the need for a programme of economic reform (remember that it did not have to take place in the way that Stalin decided). The development of the essay then looks at the aims of the plans and whether they worked. Here you should ensure that facts and figures are used sparingly – do not let them get in the way of the argument you are making and do not let them dominate your synthesis.

    I have decided to divide up the industry and agriculture plans, because I would like to say that the former was more acceptable than the latter, and that the farming reform had a greater and more devastating impact on Russian lives and culture. (Remember that part of the question asks about impact!) I want to look at impact as I go along. I think this will mean that I am more analytical, and that my argument is stronger. I also want to distinguish between short- and long-term impact – so that my conclusion can draw together several ideas that I have introduced.

## Political systems

'From each, according to his abilities. To each, according to his need.'

***Karl Marx***

'So long as the state exists there is no freedom. When there is freedom there will be no state.'

***V. I. Lenin***

## The economic situation ...

'The socialist experiment ran into trouble in Russia for reasons that Marx himself had predicted. Marx had insisted that socialism could be built only under conditions of abundance and high productivity. Without a high level of abundance, he argued, the attempt to create a more egalitarian society would impoverish as many as it would enrich. This would ensure the persistence of social and political conflict. In launching a socialist revolution in backward Russia, the Bolsheviks knew they were flouting this basic principle. they did so in the conviction that the revolution would be worldwide ... Stalinism fulfilled Marx's gloomy prediction that the attempt to build socialism under conditions of backwardness would generate violent social conflict.'

***David Christian, Imperial and Soviet Russia, Power, Privilege and the Challenge of Modernity, 1977***

### Considering the past ...

'The future is dark, the present burdensome; only the past, dead and finished, bears contemplation. Those who look on it have survived it: they are its product and its victors.'

**G. R. Elton**

### Evaluating the Red Century ...

'No matter what one thinks of Bolshevism, it is undeniable that the Russian Revolution is one of the great events of human history, and the rise of the Bolsheviki a phenomenon of worldwide importance.'

**John Reed, Ten Days that Shook the World, 1919**

'Revolutions are about people. They can radically alter the lives of millions of people. The October Revolution, one of the most important, turned Russian society upside down. One can hardly expect those who suffered as a result of it to be very charitable about its advent.'

**Martin McCauley (ed.), The Russian Revolution and the Soviet State 1917–1921, 1975**

'The inability to stop the flow of blood turned out to be a sickness not only of the last Tsarevich, but of all Russia in the twentieth century.'

**Brian Moynahan, The Russian Century, 1997**

(The heir to the throne in 1917 suffered from haemophilia.)

# *Final Review*

## HISTORIOGRAPHY AND INTERPRETATIONS

One of the purposes of this book is to try to clarify the narrative side of the Russian Revolutions, and the era of Lenin and Stalin – to lay things out for you clearly. We have made reference to 'interpretations' on a number of occasions, but what does the term mean? Interpretations are the judgements that historians make when they have a clear perspective of what happened, and some idea of why – the causes and consequences.

History is fragmentary: the what and why are not very clear, and evidence can be contradictory. An interpretation then makes a balanced suggestion as to what happened, why and what the significance of events was in the big picture. You will find some interpretations listed in the margins, and you should have begun to realise that historians can disagree with each other. Do not be afraid to make your own observations and interpretations, but be ready to back them up with an argument and evidence. The historian has to be able to support his or her conclusions and assertions.

## WHAT DO WE MEAN BY THE TERM 'HISTORIOGRAPHY'?

Historiography describes the range of interpretations of an event or period that exist. We know that historians disagree on the significance of events or personalities, and in their theories of cause and consequence. This creates the historiography of a period or place.

Writers of history can be influenced by the mood of the time, by events in their own lives or by the world around them. Some are shaped by political or moral philosophies or by the values of their period. Historians who have similar beliefs, interests and influences often show similar characteristics in their work, and are grouped together as a 'school' or 'approach' to history. For example, left-wing historians might be influenced by, and write in the style of, the Marxist interpretation of history. Historians with an interest in researching the role of women in the Soviet Union, and in looking at gender and equality issues from a feminist perspective, will reflect a women's school of history approach.

## IS IT POSSIBLE TO EVALUATE COMMUNISM IN RUSSIA YET?

In the early years after the Cold War, it might be possible to begin to look at Soviet history and distance ourselves from the preconceptions, hidden agendas, politicisation of the past and practical difficulties that were present between the Soviets and the West. Can we really give a fair account yet? It will take a considerable time before substantial research can clarify the historical record and make detailed judgements about some aspects of this troubled century.

Further work is necessary on regional issues, on the role of particular groups and sections within society, and on the experience of women and ethnic minorities.

Chris Ward, writing in 1993, comments that 'most writing [on Soviet history] has been homocentric [based on the role of men]: scant attention has been paid to women, even by socialist historians studying the working class or the peasantry. Equally the nationalities have been viewed almost exclusively in the context of state building modernisation, ideology or the purges – objects of policy rather than subjects in their own right. And the study of popular culture is only in its infancy.'

# THE GREAT DICTATORS?

Some issues may be more certain – for example, about the motives, characters and actions of many of the national figures. But perhaps not. Controversy rages about the extent to which new documents are confirming old opinions and interpretations. In 1996 Professor Richard Pipes, a popular and respected writer on Soviet affairs in the United States, reviewed a biography of Leon Trotsky by the retired Russian General, Dmitri Volkogonov. The comments made in the right-wing American's review so enraged some members of the American political Left that a strong exchange of views took place. David North, national Secretary of the Workers League and editor of *The Fourth International, the Journal of the International Committee of The Fourth International*, wrote to the *New York Times* Book Review criticising Pipes.

Clearly, political issues do still interact with our interpretation of the past.

When Lenin died in 1924, the Russian people mourned, despite the millions of deaths and the hardship caused under his leadership. History sees him as a great thinker, orator and leader, but like all individuals he is seen as imperfect. Stalin has assumed the role of bogeyman of the Communist era, and yet Lenin's Russia also saw purges and extremes of violence. Modern historians such as Chris Ward state that we must not solely judge Stalin by the standards of our time and values. He was a product of a system that he helped to create, with all the personal insecurity and ruthlessness that extreme government fosters.

On Stalin's death in 1953 it seemed clear that Communism would continue with little dramatic change, and yet Stalin was soon re-evaluated by historians, former colleagues and the Russian people as a figure to revile. Within four decades Communism in Europe had started to crumble – revolution in Prague, the collapse of East Germany, Hungary and Romania, Poland and the Czech and Slovak Republics, and even Albania, which had once chastised Russia for being revisionist. How will historians interpret the Communist era in Russia?

# MAKING JUDGEMENTS?

This book tries to remain impartial and report on historical controversies, although there are clearly occasions when there is a moral issue as well as historical disagreement amongst historians – sometimes characters in history do wrong. In early 19th century Britain, a writer and philosopher called Jeremy Bentham wrote that governments had to promote the greatest good for the greatest number of the people. This theory has been called 'utilitarianism'.

Think back to the great names of Russian and Soviet history. Were these men always following a utilitarian principle? To what extent is it acceptable to sacrifice part of the population to benefit the remainder? Philosophical issues are never easy to resolve, and certainly your writing must tread a careful line between fact and comment, analysis and judgement.

People, and history, are complex and conjure up different interpretations at different points and places in history themselves. The past is more than Gibbon's definition – the crimes, misfortunes and follies of people. It is also a study of the interaction of people, generosity, self-sacrifice and success. The story of Russia during the 20th century is one of dreams as well as of nightmares, and we should not lose track of the dream that everyone has a worth and value, and deserves a place in history.

## Current interpretations ...

'Half a century after Stalin's revolution and seventy years after the October Revolution, the Soviet Union was one of the two powers dominating the world. Like the USA, the USSR was regarded as a source of help and guidance by some countries, with fear and suspicion by others. The superpowers represented incompatible ideologies, both rooted in the nineteenth century: liberal-democratic capitalist individualism versus Marxist–Leninist state socialism.

**Tom Corfe, *Russia's Revolutions*, 1989**

'The world can sigh in relief. The idol of Communism which spread everywhere social strife, animosity, and unparalleled brutality, which instilled fear in humanity, has collapsed. It has collapsed, never to rise again.

**Boris Yeltsin**

## New interpretations ...

Sheila Fitzpatrick writes, in her discussion of the nature of revolutions, 'It is the nature of revolutions to end in disillusionment and disappointment' (*The Russian Revolution*, Opus, 1994). In many ways, there is likely to be a period of disillusionment with Soviet history. Left- and right-wing historians will look for reasons for its collapse, and may well seek to blame the corrupting influence of dictatorship and decaying ideals. In the future there will be further re-inventions and a new approach will begin. Historians from different schools of history will continue to place different emphases on events, the role of personalities and the will of the people.

### Reviewing the Red Century: cause and effect

Future historians will look back on the Russian Revolutions and the years from 1917 to 1991 in a way that we cannot. The events of the past few decades are too fresh, too unclear to be properly interpreted and explained in a historical sense. The politician Kenneth Clarke is reputed to have prevented the writers of the history national curriculum in England from including anything past 1960. Anything past 1960, he is alleged to have said, is not history; it is current affairs. Certainly, anything in recent Eastern European history still has a considerable influence on current affairs and politics. The break-up of the Soviet Union from 1991, the end of the Communist Warsaw Pact and the reunification of Germany have implications that we are yet to fully understand. We can see the cause, we can look at the immediate effects – but it is too soon to be able to judge the long-term consequences.

## AFTER STALIN

When Stalin died, he had lived a full, and perhaps rewarding, life. It was a life largely spent out of the public eye, in the world of Politburo politics and Kremlin intrigues, and masked by propaganda and myth-making. Nonetheless, we know a great deal about Stalin and the other figures of Russian history – certainly more than they expected could be possible – and yet our task of evaluating the impact of the Red Century in Russia is only just beginning. This brief section is an attempt to put the events in Soviet history after Stalin into an outline context, so that you can see what happened next. Nothing in history ever happens in isolation.

## THE LEADERSHIP

### Nikita Khrushchev (1953–1964)

Stalin was succeeded by Malenkov as Prime Minister, and Khrushchev as Secretary-General of the Communist Party. Khrushchev reduced the influence of his rivals and removed Malenkov from his post in 1955, along with other Stalinist figures by 1957.

Khrushchev denounced Stalin's harsh policies, and began a process of reducing the mechanism of the police state, releasing some political prisoners and allowing a more liberal regime. More progressive social policies were introduced, and a more relaxed atmosphere was briefly achieved. In foreign policy, Khrushchev was a great showman and he built up an image of being friendly and outgoing, travelling widely on diplomatic missions. Nonetheless, he crushed revolts in Poland and Hungary (1956) and continued to exhibit a deep mistrust of the USA and their foreign policy. Crisis points came in the early 1960s: in June 1961 the Americans backed Cuban exiles in their attempt to overthrow the Communist Cuban leader Fidel Castro, but failed dismally. Tension mounted, and was worsened when American spy planes located Soviet missiles in Cuba.

In Europe, relations were tense, especially over the division of Germany. In 1961 the Berlin Wall was erected to prevent East German citizens crossing to the West. Soviet relations with China reached a low point in 1958, when Chinese demands for economic and technological assistance from the USSR were matched by criticisms of the USSR for watering down Communism.

By the time Khrushchev was removed from office in 1964, he had tried to make the USSR more active abroad without achieving popularity at home or elsewhere. One commentator said that:

'Khrushchev had blustered across the scene like a high wind breaking up the surface but leaving the deep rooted problems untouched. Under his leadership the nation had drifted in a state of change and turmoil.'
*Ian Grey, The First Fifty Years, 1967*

Khrushchev had attempted to liberalise Soviet domestic policy, stimulate the production of consumer goods and (unsuccessfully) reform agriculture. His opponents removed him from office, and a backlash took place against many of his liberalising measures.

### Leonid Brezhnev (1964–1982)

Brezhnev was elected to be Secretary-General with Alexei Kosygin as Prime Minister. They continued many of Khrushchev's domestic policies, with a greater emphasis on the production of consumer goods. Old-style punishments for wreckers were reintroduced, together with a greater emphasis on the secret police and on repression. In foreign policy, the Soviet

Union backed regimes and Communist-led groups against groups backed by the Americans. Both used their cash and influence to carry out a bitter rivalry without directly fighting each other. Throughout the 1960s and 1970s, the Cold War was being fought in Asia and Africa, in developing countries, as the Communists and capitalists backed their own favoured factions.

In Europe, trouble again flared as Communist satellite states tried unsuccessfully to liberalise their regime: for example, in 1968 Soviet tanks were sent to Czechoslovakia to crush Alexander Dubcek's liberalising Communist regime.

Brezhnev's inactivity at home allowed the economy to grow unhindered, but his repressive policies and his failure to halt the arms race of the Cold War are major failings of his rule.

## Yuri Andropov (1982–1984) and Konstantin Chernenko (1984–1985)

Both men were elderly members of the inner circle of Soviet leaders, and neither stayed in office long enough to have a dramatic impact on politics. Their legacy was to ensure that a younger and more energetic leader was selected.

## Mikhail Gorbachev (Last Leader of the USSR, 1985–1991) and Boris Yeltsin (First Leader of the Russian Federation, 1991– )

Gorbachev was a great reformer, and his liberalisation of the USSR led to the collapse of Communism in 1991. His rival, Boris Yeltsin, stood against reactionary elements in the 1991 coup and took power. By December 1991 the Communist Party was illegal, and the USSR became the Commonwealth of Independent States, a federation of the former Soviet Republics. Since then there have been internal wars and tensions within the former USSR, and many environmental, territorial and other issues are yet to be resolved.

The history of Russia in the Gorbachev and Yeltsin years is, in itself, a fascinating story, as is the break-up of the Eastern European Communist states, and their road to economic transformation and democracy. It is a story that is by no means over.

It is too early yet to say whether the post-Communist age will lead the former Eastern Bloc successfully from Soviet dictatorship to democracy and capitalism. One can only hope that the spirit of resilience and patience that enabled the Soviet people to survive the Communist era will bring them, and their neighbours, into the 21st century successfully.

| Peaceful coexistence | Cold War | Détente | Disarmament talks | | |
|---|---|---|---|---|---|
| Liberalisation | Economic stagnation and fewer civil rights | | Reform | | |
| 1953 | 1964 | | 1982 1984 1985 | | 1991 |
| Stalin / Collective leadership / Khruschev | Collective leadership / Brezhnev | | Andropov / Chernenko | Gorbachev | Yeltsin |
| 1955 1960 | 1970 | 1980 | | 1990 | CONFEDERATION OF INDEPENDENT STATES (CIS) |
| UNION OF SOVIET SOCIALIST REPUBLICS (USSR) | | | | | |

*Timeline: Soviet and Eastern European history, 1953–1998*

### The end ... or the beginning?

At the start of this book we quoted Edward Gibbon's opinion of history, which is little more than the register of the crimes, follies and misfortunes of man. Russian history is certainly dominated by the actions of a small number of individuals, but it is more than that. Look beyond the ideology, ambition, autocracy and extremism. Look at the dream, the successes against the odds, and appreciate the moments of victory and heroism, of bravery and principle – it is a fascinating story, and well worth investigating further.

# Index